Essential Cybersecurity Science

Build, Test, and Evaluate Secure Systems

Josiah Dykstra

Beijing · Boston · Farnham · Sebastopol · Tokyo

Essential Cybersecurity Science

by Josiah Dykstra

Printed in the United States of America.

Published by O'Reilly Media, Inc., 1005 Gravenstein Highway North, Sebastopol, CA 95472.

O'Reilly books may be purchased for educational, business, or sales promotional use. Online editions are also available for most titles (*http://safaribooksonline.com*). For more information, contact our corporate/institutional sales department: 800-998-9938 or *corporate@oreilly.com*.

Editors: Rachel Roumeliotis and Heather Scherer	**Indexer:** Lucie Haskins
Production Editor: Melanie Yarbrough	**Interior Designer:** David Futato
Copyeditor: Gillian McGarvey	**Cover Designer:** Ellie Volkhausen
Proofreader: Susan Moritz	**Illustrator:** Rebecca Demarest

December 2015:   First Edition

Revision History for the First Edition
2015-12-01: First Release
2016-03-18: Second Release

See *http://oreilly.com/catalog/errata.csp?isbn=0636920037231* for release details.

978-1-491-92094-7

[LSI]

Table of Contents

Preface

Who This Book Is For

Science applies to many areas of cybersecurity, and the target audience for this book is broad and varied. This book is particularly for developers, engineers, and entrepreneurs who are building and evaluating cybersecurity hardware and software solutions. Among that group, it is for infosec practitioners such as forensic investigators, malware analysts, and other cybersecurity specialists who use, build, and test new tools for their daily work. Some will have programming experience, others a working knowledge of various security tools (EnCase for forensics, Wireshark for network analysis, IDA Pro for reverse engineering, and so on). The scientific method can be applied to all of these disciplines. Cybersecurity science can be applied to everyday problems, including:

- Testing for bugs in your new smartphone game
- Defending corporate security choices given a limited budget
- Convincing people that your new security product is better than the competition's
- Balancing intrusion detection accuracy and performance

The core audience is information security professionals who have worked in the field for 5–10 years, who are becoming experts in their craft and field, who are not formally trained in or exposed to scientific investigation in their daily lives, and who desire to learn a new approach that supplements and improves their work. I want you to walk away from this book knowing how to conduct scientific experiments on your everyday tools and procedures, and knowing that after conducting such experiments, you have done your job more securely, more accurately, and more effectively.

This book is not intended to turn you into a scientist, but it will introduce you to the discipline of scientific thinking. For those new to the field, including students of cybersecurity, this book will help you learn about the scientific method as it applies to cybersecurity and how you can conduct scientific experiments in your new profession. For nondevelopers involved in cybersecurity, such as IT security administrators who use, evaluate, buy, and recommend security solutions for the enterprise, this book will help you conduct hands-on experiments and interpret the scientific claims of others.

What This Book Contains

The first three chapters contain general information about the scientific method as it applies across many domains of cybersecurity. They cover the basic tenets of science, the need for science in cybersecurity, and the methodology for scientific investigation. Chapter 1 covers the scientific method and the importance of science to cybersecurity. Chapter 2 discusses the prerequisites needed to conduct cybersecurity experiments, from asking good questions to putting the results to work. It also includes a checklist to help you construct your own experiments. Chapter 3 includes practical details about experimentation including test environments and open datasets.

The remaining chapters are organized into standalone, domain-specific topics. You can read them individually, although new scientific topics and techniques in these chapters are applicable to other domains. These chapters explore how the scientific method can be applied to the specific topics and challenges of each domain. Each topic chapter contains an overview of the scientific pursuits in that domain, one instructive example of a scientific experiment in that field, introduction of an analysis method (which can be applied to other domains), and a practical example of a simple, introductory experiment in that field that walks through the application of the scientific method.

- Chapter 4 is about cybersecurity science for software assurance, including fuzzing and adversarial models.

- Chapter 5 covers intrusion detection and incident response, and introduces error rates (false positives and false negatives) and performance/scalability/stress testing.

- Chapter 6 focuses on the application of science to cyber situational awareness, especially using machine learning and big data.

- Chapter 7 covers cryptography and the benefits and limitations of provably secure cybersecurity.

- Chapter 8 is about digital forensics including scientific reproducibility and repeatability.

- Chapter 9, on malware analysis, introduces game theory and malware clustering.

- Chapter 10 discusses building and evaluating dependable systems with security engineering.

- Chapter 11 covers empirical experimentation for human-computer interaction and security usability.

- Chapter 12 includes techniques for the experimental evaluation of security visualization.

Appendix A provides some additional information about evaluating scientific claims, especially from vendors, and how people can be misled, manipulated, or deceived by real or bogus science. There is also a list of clarifying questions that you can use with salespeople, researchers, and product developers to probe the methodology they used.

Conventions Used in This Book

The following typographical conventions are used in this book:

Italic
> Indicates new terms, URLs, email addresses, filenames, and file extensions.

`Constant width`
> Used for program listings, as well as within paragraphs to refer to program elements such as variable or function names, databases, data types, environment variables, statements, and keywords.

`Constant width bold`
> Shows commands or other text that should be typed literally by the user.

`Constant width italic`
> Shows text that should be replaced with user-supplied values or by values determined by context.

> This element signifies a tip or suggestion.

> This element signifies a general note.

This element indicates a warning or caution.

Safari® Books Online

 Safari Books Online (*www.safaribooksonline.com*) is an on-demand digital library that delivers expert content in both book and video form from the world's leading authors in technology and business.

Technology professionals, software developers, web designers, and business and creative professionals use Safari Books Online as their primary resource for research, problem solving, learning, and certification training.

Safari Books Online offers a range of plans and pricing for enterprise, government, and education, and individuals.

Members have access to thousands of books, training videos, and prepublication manuscripts in one fully searchable database from publishers like O'Reilly Media, Prentice Hall Professional, Addison-Wesley Professional, Microsoft Press, Sams, Que, Peachpit Press, Focal Press, Cisco Press, John Wiley & Sons, Syngress, Morgan Kaufmann, IBM Redbooks, Packt, Adobe Press, FT Press, Apress, Manning, New Riders, McGraw-Hill, Jones & Bartlett, Course Technology, and hundreds more. For more information about Safari Books Online, please visit us online.

How to Contact Us

Please address comments and questions concerning this book to the publisher:

O'Reilly Media, Inc.
1005 Gravenstein Highway North
Sebastopol, CA 95472
800-998-9938 (in the United States or Canada)
707-829-0515 (international or local)
707-829-0104 (fax)

We have a web page for this book, where we list errata, examples, and any additional information. You can access this page at *http://bit.ly/essential-cybersecurity-science*.

To comment or ask technical questions about this book, send email to *bookquestions@oreilly.com*.

For more information about our books, courses, conferences, and news, see our website at *http://www.oreilly.com*.

Find us on Facebook: *http://facebook.com/oreilly*

Follow us on Twitter: *http://twitter.com/oreillymedia*

Watch us on YouTube: *http://www.youtube.com/oreillymedia*

Disclaimer

The views expressed in this book are those of the author alone. Reference to any specific commercial products, process, or service by trade name, trademark, manufacturer, or otherwise, do not necessarily constitute or imply endorsement, recommendation, or favoring by the United States Government or the Department of Defense.

Acknowledgments

My sincere thanks go to Rachel Roumeliotis, Heather Scherer, Nan Barber, and the entire team at O'Reilly for helping me through the editing and publication process. I am grateful to the brilliant and honest technical reviewers, Michael Collins and Matt Georgy, who improved many facets of the book. Thank you to my friends and colleagues who provided feedback and support on this project: Janelle Weidner Romano, Tim Leschke, Celeste Lyn Paul, Greg Shannon, Brian Sherlock, Chris Toombs, Tom Walcott, and Cathy Wu. I also wish to thank the community of friends, colleagues, and strangers that I interacted with at conferences, meetings, and workshops on cybersecurity science over the past few years, especially LASER, CSET, and HoTSoS. These conversations helped influence and contribute to many of the ideas in this book. Most importantly, thank you to my wife Alicia for her love and encouragement in this project and in all things.

## CHAPTER 1

Introduction to Cybersecurity Science

This chapter will introduce the concept—and importance—of cybersecurity science, the scientific method, the relationship of cybersecurity theory and practice, and high-level topics that relate to science, including human factors and metrics.

Whether you're a student, software developer, forensic investigator, network administrator, or have any other role in providing cybersecurity, this book will teach you the relevant scientific principles and flexible methodologies for effective cybersecurity. *Essential Cybersecurity Science* focuses on real-world applications of science to your role in providing cybersecurity. You'll learn how to conduct your own experiments that can evaluate assurances of security.

Let me offer a few reasons why science is worth the trouble.

- **Science is respected**. A majority of the population sees value in scientific inquiry and scientific results. Advertisers appeal to it all the time, even if the science is nonsensical or made up. People will respect you and your work in cybersecurity if you demonstrate good science. "In the past few years, there has been significant interest in promoting the idea of applying scientific principles to information security," said one report.[1] Scientific research can help convince your audience about the value of a result.

- **Science is sexy**. In addition to respect, many nonscientists desire to understand and be part of a field they admire. Once perceived as dry, boring, and geeky, science is becoming a thing of admiration, and more and more people want to be identified with it.

---

1 Barriers to the Science of Security. (*http://nsf.gov/events/event_summ.jsp?cntn_id=123377*)

- **Science provokes curiosity**. Information security (infosec) professionals are curious. They ask good questions and crave information, as evidenced by the increasing value being placed on data science. Science is a vehicle for information, and answers stimulate more questions. Scientific inquiry brings a deeper understanding about the cybersecurity domain.

- **Science creates and improves products**. In the commercial space, the market drives cybersecurity. Scientific knowledge can improve existing products and lead to groundbreaking innovation and applications. For infosec decision-makers, the scientific method can make product evaluations defensible and efficient.

- **Science advances knowledge**. Science is one of the primary ways that humans unearth new knowledge about the world. Participants in science have the opportunity to contribute to the body of human understanding and advance the state of the art. In cybersecurity in particular, science will help prove practices and techniques that work, moving us away from today's practice of cybersecurity "folk wisdom."

Scientific experimentation and inquiry reveal opportunities to optimize and create more secure cyber solutions. For instance, mathematics alone can help cryptographers determine how to design more secure crypto algorithms, but mathematics does not govern the process of how to design a useful network mapping visualization. Visualization requires experimentation and repeatable user studies. Validation in this context is more like justification for design choices. What is the optimal sampling rate for NetFlow in my situation? Trying to answer that question and maximize the validity of the answer is a scientific endeavor. Furthermore, you can learn and apply lessons from what others have done in the past.

What Is Cybersecurity Science?

Cybersecurity science is an important aspect of the understanding, development, and practice of cybersecurity. *Cybersecurity* is a broad category, covering the technology and practices used to protect computer networks, computers, and data from harm. People throughout industry, academia, and government all use formal and informal science to create and expand cybersecurity knowledge. As a discipline, the field of cybersecurity requires authentic knowledge to explore and reason about the "how and why" we build or deploy security controls.

When I talk about applying science and the scientific method to cybersecurity, I mean leveraging the body of knowledge about cybersecurity (science) and a particular set of techniques for testing a hypothesis against empirical reality (the scientific method).

The Many Ways to Obtain Knowledge

Scientific investigation is not the only way to obtain knowledge. Among the non-scientific methods can be common sense, intuition, and deduction.

Common sense describes knowledge that most people have in common, often relating to human experiences. Intuition is the acquisition of knowledge without conscious reasoning. Deduction uses given premises to reach conclusions (e.g., All men are mortal. Einstein is a man. Therefore, Einstein is mortal). Mathematics is deductive, because axioms are assumed to be true without being tested.

In his book *What Engineers Know and How They Know It*, Walter Vincenti identified six categories of engineering knowledge that seem to apply to cybersecurity:

- Fundamental design concepts
- Criteria and specifications
- Theoretical tools
- Quantitative data
- Practical considerations
- Design instrumentalities

Another naive, but sadly common, method of advancing cybersecurity science is by uninformed and untested guessing. We guess about what users want tools to do. We guess about what to buy and how to deploy cybersecurity solutions. Guessing is uninformed and ineffective, and while it may appear to advance security, it is difficult to defend and often fails miserably.

Unfortunately, science has a reputation for being stuffy and cold, and something that only people in white lab coats are excited about. As a cybersecurity practitioner, think of science as a way to explore your curiosity, an opportunity to discover something unexpected, and a tool to improve your work.

You benefit every day from the experimentation and scientific investigation done by people in cybersecurity. To cite a few examples:

- Microsoft Research (*http://research.microsoft.com/en-us/about/techtransfer/ product-development-contributions-2011.aspx*) provides key security advances for Microsoft products and services, including algorithms to detect tens of millions of malicious Hotmail accounts.

- Government and private researchers created Security-enhanced Linux (*https://www.nsa.gov/research/selinux/contrib.shtml*).
- Research at Google (*http://bit.ly/1SlAKxW*) helps improve products such as Chrome browser security and YouTube video fingerprinting.
- Symantec Research Labs (*http://symc.ly/1SlAWNU*) has contributed new algorithms, performance speedups, and products for the company.

Cybersecurity is an *applied science*. That is, people in the field often apply known facts and scientific discoveries to create useful applications, often in the form of technology. Other forms of science include natural science (e.g., biology), formal science (e.g., statistics), and social science (e.g., economics). Cybersecurity overlaps and is influenced by connections with social sciences such as economics, sociology, and criminology.

What About the Art of Cybersecurity?

You might be asking yourself, "Science is great, but what about the art of cybersecurity?" The word *art* connotes skill in doing something, especially as the result of knowledge or practice. There is art in becoming an expert at reverse engineering and malware analysis because skill, practice, and experience make practitioners better at those tasks.

Changing passwords every 30 or 90 days is an example of cybersecurity folk wisdom, or something people consider a "best practice" to use as a default policy, particularly people who lack the data or training for their own risk assessment. However, the art and practice of password management leads to different conclusions. Password strength is based on mathematical properties of the encryption algorithms used and the strength of modern computers. There is debate even among the world's infosec experts about the benefits of website "password meters" and password expiration.

Art is one way to handle the ever-changing assumptions and landscape in cybersecurity. Take *address space layout randomization* (ASLR), for example. ASLR is a technique of randomizing code in memory to prevent buffer overflow attacks. Researchers have been studying the effectiveness and shortcomings of this technique for years. One frequently cited paper from 2004 experimentally showed a way to de-randomize memory even under ASLR. This example illustrates the change in knowledge over time.[2]

---

2 Hovav Shacham, Matthew Page, Ben Pfaff, Eu-Jin Goh, Nagendra Modadugu, and Dan Boneh. 2004. "On the effectiveness of address-space randomization." In *Proceedings of the 11th ACM Conference on Computer and Communications Security* (CCS '04). ACM, New York, NY, USA, 298-307.

Like applied science, cybersecurity science often takes the form of applied research—the goal of the work is to discover how to meet a specific need. For example, if you wanted to figure out how to tune your intrusion detection system, that could be an applied research project.

The Importance of Cybersecurity Science

Every day, you as developers and security practitioners deal with uncertainty, unknowns, choices, and crises that could be informed by scientific methods. You might also face very real adversaries who are hard to reason about. According to a report on the science of cybersecurity, "There is every reason to believe that the traditional domains of experimental and theoretical inquiry apply to the study of cybersecurity. The highest priority should be assigned to establishing research protocols to enable reproducible experiments."[3]

To get started, look at the following examples of how cybersecurity science could be applied to practical cybersecurity situations:

- Your job is defending your corporate network and you have a limited budget. You've been convinced by a new security concept called Moving Target Defense, which says that controlling change across multiple system dimensions increases uncertainty and complexity for attackers. Game theory is a scientific technique well-suited to modeling the arms race between attackers and defenders, and quantitatively evaluating dependability and security. So you could try setting up an experiment to determine how often you'll have to apply moving target defense if you think the attacker will try to attack you 10 times a day.

- As a malware analyst, you are responsible for writing intrusion detection system (IDS) signatures to identify and block malware from entering your network. You want the signature to be accurate, but IDS performance is also important. If you knew how to model the load, you could write a program to determine the number of false negatives for a given load.

- You've written a new program that could revolutionize desktop security. You want to convince people that it's better than today's antivirus. You decide to run analysis to determine whether people will buy your software, by comparing the number of compromises when using your product versus antivirus and also factoring in the cost of the two products. This is a classical statistical gotcha because you've introduced two incompatible variables (compromises detected and dollars).

---

3 *Science of Cyber Security*, MITRE Report JSR-10-102, November 2010, *http://fas.org/irp/agency/dod/jason/cyber.pdf*.

- You've developed a smartphone game that's taking off in the marketplace. However, users have started complaining about the app crashing randomly. You would be wise to run an experiment with a random "monkey" that ran your app over and over, pressing buttons in different sequences to help identify which code path leads to the crash.

Cybersecurity requires defenders to think about worst-case behaviors and rare events, and that can be challenging to model realistically. Cybersecurity comprises large, complex, decentralized systems—and scientific inquiry dislikes complexity and chaos. Cybersecurity must deal with inherently multiparty environments, with many users and systems. Accordingly, it becomes difficult to pinpoint the important variable(s) in an experiment with these complex features.

Cybersecurity is complex because it is constantly changing. As soon as you think you've addressed a problem, the problem or the environment changes. Amazon, which has reportedly sold as many as 306 items per second, commissioned a study to determine how many different shaped and sized boxes they needed. The mostly mathematical study went on for over a year and the team produced a recommendation. The following day, Amazon launched an identical study to re-examine the exact same problem because buyers' habits had changed and people were buying different sized and shaped goods. Cybersecurity, like shopping habits, is a constantly changing problem, as evidenced by dynamic Internet routing and the unpredictable demand on Internet servers and services.

Science isn't just about solving problems by confirming hypotheses; science is also about falsifiability. Instead of proving a scientific hypothesis correct, the idea is to disprove a hypothesis. This scientific philosophy came in Karl Popper's 1935 book *The Logic of Scientific Discovery*. Popper used falsifiability as the demarcation criterion for science but noted that science often proceeds based on claims or conjectures that cannot (easily) be verified. If something is falsifiable, that doesn't mean that it is false. It means that if the hypothesis were false, then you could demonstrate its falsehood. For example, if a newspaper offers the hypothesis "China is the biggest cyber threat," that claim is nonfalsifiable because you can't prove it wrong. Perhaps it is based on undisclosed evidence. If the statement is wrong, all you will ever find is an absence of evidence. There is no way to empirically test the hypothesis.

Central motivations for the scientific method are to uncover new truths and to root out error, common goals shared with cybersecurity. Science has been revealing insights into "what if" questions for thousands of years. Businesses need new products and innovations to stay alive, and science can produce amazing and sometimes unexpected results to create and improve technology and cybersecurity. Science can also provide validation for the work you do by showing—even proving—that your ideas and solutions are better than others. If you choose to present your findings in papers or at conferences, you also receive external validation from your peers and contribute to the global body of knowledge.

Think about how much science plays a part at Google, even aside from security. The 1998 paper Google published on the PageRank algorithm described a novel idea that launched a $380 billion company. Today, Google researchers publish dozens of papers on security (*http://research.google.com/pubs/SecurityCryptographyandPrivacy.html*) every year and those results inform security in their products and services, from Android to Gmail. Scientific advances conducted inside and outside the company undoubtedly save and make money for Google.

Lastly, learning science consists, in part, of learning the language of science. Once you learn the language, you'll be better equipped to understand scientific conversations and papers. You will also have the ability to more clearly communicate your results to others, and it's more likely that other amateur and professional scientists will respect your work.

The Scientific Method

The scientific method is a structured way of investigating the world. This group of techniques can be used to gain knowledge, study the state of the world, correct errors in current knowledge, and integrate facts. Importantly for us, the scientific method contributes to a theoretical and practical understanding of cybersecurity.

Our modern understanding of the scientific method stems from Francis Bacon's *Novum Organum* (1620) and the work of Descartes, though others have refined the process since then. The Oxford English Dictionary defines the scientific method as "a method of observation or procedure based on scientific ideas or methods; specifically an empirical method that has underlain the development of natural science since the 17th century." An *empirical method* is one in which the steps are based on observation, investigation, or experimentation.

At its heart, the scientific method contains only five essential elements:

1. Formulating a question from previous observations, measurements, or experiments

2. Induction and formulation of hypotheses

3. Making predictions from the hypotheses

4. Experimental testing of the predictions

5. Analysis and modification of the hypotheses

These steps are said to be *systematic*. That is to say, they are conducted according to a plan or organized method. If you jump around the steps in an unplanned way, you will have violated the scientific method. In Chapter 2 we will discuss how to do each of these five steps.

There are also five governing principles of the scientific method. These principles are:

1. **Objective**. A fair, objective experiment is free from bias and considers all the data (or a representative sample), not just data that validates your hypothesis.

2. **Falsifiable**. It must be possible to show that your hypothesis is false.

3. **Reproducible**. It must be possible for you or others to reproduce your results.[4]

4. **Predictable**. The results from the scientific method can be used to predict future outcomes in other situations.

5. **Verifiable**. Nothing is accepted until verified through adequate observations or experiments.

It's interesting that the scientific method isn't on the computer science curriculum in graduate school or computer security professional certifications. Many students and professionals haven't considered the scientific method since grade school and no longer remember how to apply it to their profession. However, the problem may be systemic. Take performance, for example. Say you have a malware detection tool and want to analyze 1,000 files. A theoretical computer scientist might look at your malware detection algorithm and say, "the asymptotic bounds of this algorithm are $O(n^2)$ time," meaning it belongs to a group of algorithms whose performance corresponds to the square of the size of the input. Informative, huh? It might be, but it masks implementation details that actually matter to the amount of wall clock time the algorithm takes in practice.

There are many research designs to choose from in the scientific method. The one you pick will be primarily based on the information you want to collect, but also on other factors such as cost. This book mainly focuses on experimentation, but other research methods are shown in Table 1-1.

Table 1-1. Types of output for various research methods

Research method	Aim of the study
Case study	Observe and describe
Survey	Observe and describe
Natural environment observation	Observe and describe
Longitudinal study	Predict
Observation study	Predict

---

4 Reproducibility is not the same as *repeatability* or *replicability*.

Research method	Aim of the study
Field experiment	Determine causes
Double-blind experiment	Determine causes
Literature review	Explain

The way you approach cybersecurity science depends on you and your situation. What if you don't have the time or resources to do precise scientific experiments? Is that OK? It probably depends on the circumstances. If you build software that is used in hospitals or nuclear command and control, I hope that science is an important part of the process. Scientists often talk about *scientific rigor*. Rigor is related to thoroughness, carefulness, and accuracy. Rigor is a commitment to the scientific method, especially in paying attention to detail and being unbiased in the work.

Cybersecurity Theory and Practice

"In theory, there is no difference between theory and practice. In practice, there is."[5] So goes a quote once overheard at a computer science conference. The contention of theory versus practice long predates cybersecurity. The argument goes that practitioners don't understand fundamentals, leading to suboptimal practices, and theorists are out of touch with real-world practice.

Research and science often emerge following practical developments. "The steam engine is a perfect example," writes Dr. Henry Petroski. "It existed well before there was a science of thermodynamics to explain what was happening from a theoretical point of view. The Wright Brothers designed a plane before there was a theory of aerodynamics." Cybersecurity may follow a similar trajectory, with empiricists running a bit ahead of theorists.

The application of theory into practice has direct impact on our lives. Consider approaches to protecting a system from denial-of-service attacks. In theory, it is impossible to distinguish between legitimate network traffic and malicious traffic because malicious traffic can imitate legitimate traffic so effectively. In practice, an administrator may find a pattern or fingerprint in attack traffic allowing her to block only the malicious traffic.

One reason for the disconnect between theory and practice in cybersecurity is that there are few axioms in security. Despite decades of work in cybersecurity, the community has failed to uncover the building blocks that you might expect from a mature field. In 2011, the US government published "Trustworthy Cyberspace: Strategic Plan for the Federal Cybersecurity Research and Development Program" (*http://1.usa.gov/*

---

5 *Pascal: An Introduction to the Art and Science of Programming* by Walter J. Savitch, 1984.

1SlC4Rw). As a result of this strategy, the government created the Science of Security Virtual Organization (SoS VO) (*http://cps-vo.org/group/SoS*) to research "first principles and the fundamental building blocks for security and trustworthiness." The NSA now funds academic research groups called "lablets" (*https://www.nsa.gov/public_info/press_room/2014/lablets.shtml*) to conduct research aimed at "establishing scientific principles upon which to base trust in security" and "to bring scientific rigor to research in the cybersecurity domain." This work aims to improve cybersecurity theory, which will hopefully in turn translate into practical cybersecurity implementations.

 Axioms are assumptions which are generally accepted as truth without proof. The mathematical axiom of transitivity says if x=y and y=z then x=z.

Pseudoscience

A word of caution: science can be used for good, but it can also be deceiving if misused, misapplied, or misunderstood. *Pseudoscience*, on the other hand, is a claim or belief that is falsely presented or mistakenly regarded as science. Theories about the Bermuda Triangle are pseudoscience because they are heavily dependent on assumptions. Beware of misinterpretation and inflation of scientific findings. Popular culture was largely misled by the media hype over the "Mozart effect," which stemmed from a paper showing increased test scores in students who listened to a Mozart sonata.

Michael Gordin, a Princeton historian of science, wrote in his book *The Pseudoscience Wars* (University of Chicago Press, 2012), "No one in the history of the world has ever self-identified as a pseudoscientist." Pseudoscience is something that we recognize after the work has been done. You should learn to recognize the markers of pseudoscience in other people's work and in your own.

For more cautionary notes on scientific claims, especially in marketing, see Appendix A.

Human Factors

Science is a human pursuit. Even when humans are not the object of scientific investigation, as they often are in biology or psychology, humans are the ones conducting all scientific inquiry including cybersecurity. The 2015 Verizon Data Breach Investigations Report pointed out that "the common denominator across the top four [incident] patterns—accounting for nearly 90% of all incidents—is people." This section introduces the high-level roles for humans in cybersecurity science and the important concept of recognizing human bias in science.

Roles Humans Play in Cybersecurity Science

Humans play a role in cybersecurity science in at least four ways:

- **Humans as developers and designers**. We will be talking a lot about cybersecurity practitioners in their roles thinking and acting as *scientists*.

- **Humans as users and consumers**. Humans as users and consumers often throw a wrench into cybersecurity. Users are commonly described as the weakest link in cybersecurity.

- **Humans as orchestrators and practitioners**. Our goal is to defend a network, data, or users, and we decide how to achieve the desired goal. Defenders must be knowledgeable of the environment, the tools at their disposal, and the state of security at a given time. Human defenders bring their own limitations to cyber defense, including their incomplete picture of the environment and their human biases.

- **Humans as active adversaries**. Human adversaries can be unpredictable, inconsistent, and irrational. They are difficult to attribute definitively, and they masquerade and hide easily online. Worse, the best human adversaries abandon specific attacks more quickly than defenders like you can discover them. Scientific inquiry in chemistry and physics have no analogous opponent.

 For a very long time, scientific inquiry was a solo activity. Experiments were done by individuals, and papers were published by a single author. However, by 2015, 90% of all science publications were written by two or more authors.[6] Today there is too much knowledge for one person to possess on his or her own. Collaboration and diversity of thought and skill make scientific results more interesting and more useful. I strongly encourage you to collaborate in your pursuit of science, and especially with people of different skills.

Human Cognitive Biases

Cognitive errors and human cognitive biases have the potential to greatly affect objective scientific study and results. *Bias* is an often misused term that when used correctly, describes irrational, systematic errors that deviate from rational decisions and cause inaccurate results. Bias is not the same as incompetence or corruption,

---

6 *Enhancing the Effectiveness of Team Science*, Nancy J. Cooke and Margaret L. Hilton (Eds.), *http://www.nap.edu/catalog/19007/enhancing-the-effectiveness-of-team-science*, 2015.

though those also interfere with neutral scientific inquiry. Below are three biases that are especially useful to beware of as you think about science.

Confirmation bias is the human tendency toward searching for or interpreting information in a way that confirms one's preconceptions, beliefs, or hypotheses, leading to statistical errors. This bias is often unconscious and unintentional rather than the result of deliberate deception. Remember that scientific thinking should seek and consider evidence that supports a hypothesis as well as evidence that falsifies the hypothesis. To avoid confirmation bias, try to keep an open mind and look into surprising results if they arise. Don't be afraid to prove yourself wrong. Confirmation bias prevents us from finding unbiased scientific truths, and contributes to overconfidence.

Daniel Kahneman, author of *Thinking Fast and Slow*, uses the acronym WYSIATI, for "what you see is all there is," to describe *overconfidence bias*. Kahneman says that "we often fail to allow for the possibility that evidence that should be critical to our judgment is missing—what we see is all there is." Without conscious care, there is a natural tendency to deal with the limited information you have as if it were all there is to know.

Cybersecurity is shaped in many ways by our previous experiences and outcomes. For example, looking back after a cybersecurity incident, our CEO might assign a higher probability that we "should have known" compared to the choices made before the incident occurred. *Hindsight bias* leads people to say "I knew that would happen" even when new information distorts an original thought. Hindsight also causes us to undervalue the element of surprise of scientific findings.

As you pursue science and scientific experimentation, keep biases in mind and continually ask yourself whether or not you think a bias is affecting your scientific processes or outcomes.

The Role of Metrics

It's easy to make a mental mistake by substituting metrics for science. Managers like metrics—the analysis of measurements over time—because they think these numbers alone allow them to determine whether the organization is secure or succeeding. Sometimes metrics really are called for. However, counting the number of security incidents at your company is not necessarily an indication of how secure or insecure the company is. Determining the percentage of weak passwords for your users is a metric but not also a scientific inquiry. As we will see in Chapter 2, hypotheses are testable proposed explanations like "people take more risks online than in their physical lives."

Don't get me wrong: most experiments measure something! Metrics can be part of the scientific process if they are used to test a hypothesis. The topic of security metrics may also be the foundation for scientific exploration. The point is not to be fooled by believing that metrics alone can be substituted for science. To learn more about the active field of security metrics, visit SecurityMetrics.org, which hosts an active mailing list and annual conference.

Conclusion

The key concepts and takeaways about the scientific method presented in this chapter and used throughout the book are:

- Cybersecurity science is an important aspect of the understanding, development, and practice of cybersecurity.
- Scientific experimentation and inquiry reveal opportunities to optimize and create more secure cyber solutions.
- The scientific method contains five essential elements: ask a good question, formulate hypotheses, make predictions, experimentally test the predictions, analyze the results.
- Experiments must be objective, falsifiable, reproducible, predictable, and verifiable.
- The human elements of cybersecurity science are critical to designing accurate and unbiased experiments and to maximizing the practical usefulness of experiments.

References

- William I. B. Beveridge. *The Art of Scientific Investigation* (Caldwell, NJ: Blackburn Press, 2004)
- Lorraine Daston and Elizabeth Lunbeck (eds). *Histories of Scientific Observation* (Chicago: University of Chicago Press, 2011)
- Richard Feynman. *The Pleasure of Finding Things Out* (*http://www.cs.virginia.edu/~robins/YouAndYourResearch.html*) (2005)
- Hugh G. Gauch, Jr. *Scientific Method in Brief* (Cambridge: Cambridge University Press, 2012)
- Richard Hamming. *You and Your Research (http://www.cs.virginia.edu/~robins/YouAndYourResearch.html)* (1986)
- International Workshop on Foundations & Practice of Security

- Roy Maxion. *Making Experiments Dependable*, Dependable and Historic Computing, ser. Lecture Notes in Computer Science, vol. 6875, pp. 344–357 (Heidelberg: Springer-Verlag, 2011)

## CHAPTER 2

Conducting Your Own Cybersecurity Experiments

This chapter delves deeper into the specific steps of the scientific method. Recall that there are five essential elements: asking a question, formulating a hypothesis, making predictions, experimental testing, and analysis. These details will help as you think about using the scientific method in your own situation. After seeing them described here, you'll apply these steps in practice in the subsequent chapters.

Asking Good Questions and Formulating Hypotheses

Formulating a good question might sound easy, but it can often be harder than it sounds. Most infosec professionals see problems that need solving every day, even if they don't keep track of them. Trying to think of a problem on the spot can be especially challenging. An economist friend of mine prefers to look for problems in proverbs. To create experimental questions, he asks *when is it the case* that "when the cat's away, the mice will play" or "don't put the cart before the horse?" These can help get you thinking about challenging the folk wisdom of cybersecurity.

Creating a Hypothesis

A hypothesis is a statement and suggested explanation. Based on this statement, you will use scientific experimentation, investigation, or observation to show support or rejection for the hypothesis. A hypothesis is temporary and unproven, but something you believe to be true. The hypothesis must be testable, and experiments can help you decide whether or not your hypothesis is true.

Consider the following example. You're interested in building a scalable automated malware analysis solution. In order to test scalability, you ask yourself, "how quickly can my solution analyze 100 files to determine if they are malicious?" This is a reasonable question and one that will help you understand and improve your product. However, it's not a scientific hypothesis because the question isn't a testable statement. Assume you've been working on your product for a while and know that you can analyze one or two files in less than 30 seconds.

Now try making the question testable. Here is a modified version of the question: "Can my solution analyze 100 files in 10 minutes?" This is now a testable proposition. It also has nice properties like the ability to prove it false, and the ability for other people to reproduce the test. What this version lacks are independent and dependent variables. The independent variable is the one single thing you change during the experiment, and the dependent variable is the thing you monitor for impact depending on changes to the independent variable. So, hypotheses can be written as if-then statements in the form "If we change this independent variable, then this dependent variable also changes."

With this formula in mind, here is a better statement of our hypothesis: "If I use one server, my solution can analyze 100 files in 10 minutes." This is your educated guess about how many files you can analyze based on previous observations. Not only is it testable, reproducible, and falsifiable, but it has an independent variable (one server) and a dependent variable (the number of files analyzed in 10 minutes). Now you have a well-formulated hypothesis.

 Don't think of a hypothesis purely as a guess. A guess has no knowledge or observation to back it up, whereas a hypothesis is based on previous observations, measurements, or experiments. You should also be careful about creating a hypothesis that you just *want* to be true. This bias would threaten the impartiality of the scientific method.

When you read scientific papers, you may occasionally find references to the *null hypothesis*. The null hypothesis, often written as H_0, is the claim that there is no relationship between two variables. When used, the null hypothesis is offered with an alternative hypothesis called H_1. The null hypothesis is assumed to be true, and you must show evidence to prove a relationship that rejects or disproves the null hypothesis. For example, you may propose null and alternative hypotheses such as:

H_0

Malware families exhibit no human-discernable visual similarities when visualized by our solution.

H_1

Malware images belonging to the same family exhibit human-discernable visual similarities in layout and texture.

Success in the scientific method is accepting or rejecting *any* hypothesis.

Accepting the null hypothesis does not mean that your experiment failed! Accepting (or rejecting) any hypothesis is a result.

Care is required when wording the null and alternative hypotheses. Don't be tempted to define your null hypothesis simply as the opposite of the alternative hypothesis. Otherwise, you might create a situation where you have to reject both the null hypothesis and the alternative—you want to be able to accept one or the other. For example, say you're studying the performance gains of a new tool. You define the null hypothesis as "there is no difference in performance" and the alternative hypothesis as "there is a performance gain." However, if the tool causes a *decrease* in performance, then you've rejected both hypotheses.

Hypotheses can sometimes be obfuscated in scientific papers. You will often find that the hypothesis is implied by the solution or contribution in the paper. In Table 2-1, there are three quotes from papers in the left column, and the corresponding implied hypothesis in the right column. It is not too difficult to infer what the hypothesis was, but it is instructive as you think about how to form hypotheses. Finally, many readers of these papers are ultimately more interested in the results and an explanation of how and why those results occurred.

Table 2-1. Implied hypotheses from real papers

Paper text	Implied hypothesis
"We found that inhibitive attractors significantly reduced the likelihood that participants would (1) install software despite the presence of clues indicating that the publisher of the software might not be legitimate, (2) grant dangerously excessive permissions to an online game, and (3) fail to recognize an instruction contained within a field of a dialog that they had been habituated to ignore."[a]	Inhibitive attractors will reduce the likelihood that users will (1) install dangerous software, (2) grant dangerously excessive permissions to online games, and (3) fail to recognize instructions contained within dialogs that they have a habit of ignoring.
"Is there any hope in mitigating the amplification problem? In this paper, we aim to answer this question and tackle the problem from four different angles…Lastly, we analyze the root cause for amplification attacks: networks that allow IP address spoofing. We deploy a method to identify spoofing-enabled networks from remote and reveal up to 2,692 Autonomous Systems that lack egress filtering."[b]	The root cause for amplification attacks is networks that allow IP address spoofing.

Paper text	Implied hypothesis
"To discourage the creation of predictable passwords, vulnerable to guessing attacks, we present Telepathwords. As a user creates a password, Telepathwords makes realtime predictions for the next character that user will type… We found that participants create far fewer weak passwords using the Telepathwords-based policies than policies based only on character composition. Participants using Telepathwords were also more likely to report that the password feedback was helpful."[c]	If shown a guess as to the next character of a user's password before he or she types it, then users will create stronger passwords.

[a] Your Attention Please: Designing security-decision UIs to make genuine risks harder to ignore. (*http://bit.ly/1SIEH62*)

[b] Exit from Hell? Reducing the Impact of Amplification DDoS Attacks. (*http://bit.ly/1SIEEal*)

[c] Telepathwords: Preventing Weak Passwords by Reading Users' Minds. (*http://bit.ly/1SIEFLa*)

With a good question and well-formulated hypothesis in hand, you are ready to consider how you will test your hypothesis.

Security and Testability

How do you know if your system is secure, and what you can actually test? By now you understand the need to scientifically test assurances of security, but system security is meaningless without a statement and specification of *security*. You and your target audiences could misunderstand each other about what security means without a defined context.

One way to describe security is with a specified security policy. The security policy defines what it means to be secure for a specific system, and the goal of a policy is to achieve some security properties. For example, a policy might say that after three incorrect password attempts, the user is locked out of his or her account. For the owner of this policy, this is one specification of security that, if followed, contributes toward the security of the company. Your definition of security may differ. There are many frameworks and policy-specification languages both for formalizing policies and for formally evaluating the effects of policies.

Validation of a security policy can be accomplished with formal and experimental methods. Formal validation is based on theories, such as the Bell-La Padula confidentiality policy, which are amenable to analysis and verification. On the other hand, experimental testing can evaluate whether a security policy is needed and whether the implementation achieves the desired security property. Say your organization requires continuous monitoring of network traffic to implement a certain security policy. In a series of experiments, you could show the computational and storage load for full packet capture versus various sampling rates of NetFlow. The outcome of these experiments would be actionable information about how to balance costs and benefits in achieving the security policy.

In later chapters we will provide a variety of experiments and examples that illustrate more testable claims of security.

Designing a Fair Test

When conducting an experiment, you may do many tests. It is vital that for each test you only change one variable at a time and keep all other conditions the same. The variable in your test is the one changing factor in the experiment. This practice is key to good science, and following this practice results in a *fair test*.

 A fair test is different from a good experiment. People often use "good" in a colloquial sense to mean interesting, clever, or important. Those are fine goals, too, but are distinct from the experiment's fairness.

Imagine that you want to test the hypothesis that a particular cryptographic algorithm is faster in C than C++. If you implement the same algorithm in both languages but run one on a laptop and one on a supercomputer, that would be an unfair test because you gave an unfair advantage to the one running on the supercomputer. The only thing that should change is the programming language, and every other part of the test should be as identical as possible. Even comparing C to C++ implies different compilers, different libraries, and other differences that you may not know about. Instead, think about comparing the speed of two different crypto algorithms in a given application.

One serious problem for fair tests is inadequate data sample sizes. This happens because gathering data can be expensive (in time, money, labor, and so on) or because the scientist just didn't calculate how much data was needed. Consider an experiment to determine the effectiveness of a cybersecurity education campaign at your company. First, determine as best as possible the size of the total population. You may have to guess or approximate. Second, decide on your confidence interval (margin of error), such as ±5%. Third, decide on your desired confidence level, such as 95%. Finally, use an online sample-size calculator to determine the recommended sample size.[1] Say your company has 1,000 employees and just did a cybersecurity awareness campaign. You are asked to study whether or not the campaign was effective by surveying a sample of the employees. If you want a 5% margin of error and 95% confidence, you need a sample size of at least 278 employees.

---

1 One such sample-size calculator can be found at Creative Research Systems (*http://www.surveysystem.com/sscalc.htm*).

Statistics is a science whose scientists cannot, in general, be replaced simply by an online tool.

Getting the sample size correct gives you *statistical power*, the ability of the test to detect the relationship between the dependent and independent variables (if one exists). When your sample size is too small, the danger is that your results could be overestimates or exaggerations of the truth. On the contrary, if your sample size is very large and you are looking for tiny effects, you're *always* going to find the effect. So, calculate the right sample size in advance. Don't start with 10 employees in the cybersecurity education campaign study and keep adding more subjects until you get a statistically significant result. Also, document and publish the reasons for choosing the sample size you used. In some fields and journals, sample size is so important that it's standard practice to publish the study protocol before doing the experiment so that the scientific community can collectively validate it! Experimental protocol outside of computer science and cybersecurity is generally well defined, but could be incompatible with fast-paced developments in cybersecurity.

A problem with proper experimental construction is that you need to identify and address challenges to validity. Validity refers to the truth of the experiment's propositions, inferences, and conclusions. Could the changes in the dependent variable be caused by anything other than changes in the independent variable? This is a threat to *internal validity*. Research with a high degree of internal validity has strong evidence of causality. *External validity*, on the other hand, refers to how well your results can be generalized and applied to other situations or groups. One must often balance internal and external validity in experimental design. For some examples of threats to the validity of cybersecurity studies, see *Experimental Challenges in Cyber Security: A Story of Provenance and Lineage for Malware* by Dumitras and Neamtiu (CSET 2011).

One challenge with fair tests is that when you create a hypothesis, you make a lot of assumptions. In reality, each assumption is another hypothesis in disguise. Consider a case where university students have been the subject of a phishing attack. The IT security team gives you demographic data about the students who fell for the attack, and you want to find correlations. Were men more likely than women? Were students under age 20 more likely than students over 20? Were chemistry majors more likely than biology majors? You could conduct fair tests by measuring each variable independently. There is also a statistical method called *regression* which allows you to measure the relative contribution of several independent variables. You'll see this method in action in Chapter 10.

Analyzing Your Results

The goal of analysis is to determine if you should accept or reject your hypothesis and then to explain why. While we described analysis as the step after experimental testing, it is wise to do some analysis during experimentation and data collection. Doing so will help save time when troubleshooting problems with the experiment.

The analysis step of the scientific method is very experiment-specific. There are a few common techniques that may be applicable to your particular experiment. One technique is to literally look at the data. Constructing graphs can draw your attention to features in the data, identify unexpected results, or raise new questions. The graphs shown in Figure 2-1 helped the authors of a paper on botnets observe that "by comparing the IRC botnet submissions in the two graphs, we can observe that, in 2007, most of IRC botnets were belonging to different clusters. In 2008 instead, we still received an [*sic*] high number of IRC bots, but they were mostly polymorphic variations of the same family."

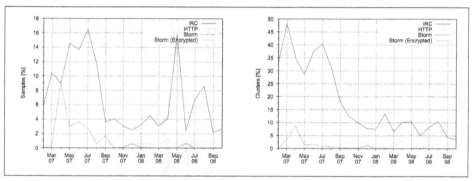

Figure 2-1. Graph of botnet submissions comparing samples to clusters (courtesy of Usenix (http://bit.ly/1SlFsMl))

Statistics is probably the most commonly used general-analysis method. It is also a rich and complex field, so we skim only the surface here to introduce general topics of use to you. All scholastic disciplines need a logic. The logic of a discipline is the methodology the discipline uses to say that something is correct, and statistics is one such set of rules. Descriptive statistics describe the basic features of a collection of data, such as the mean, median, mode, standard deviation (or variance), and frequency. Inferential statistics uses samples of a larger dataset to infer conclusions about the larger population. Examples of inferential statistics are Bayesian inference, comparison to specific distributions (such as a chi-square test), grouping by categories (statistical classification), and regression (estimating relationships between variables). Table 2-2 illustrates various distributions of data, and a corresponding analysis method.

Table 2-2. Correspondence between analytical goals, graphical data, and analytical methods

Analytical goal	Data visualization	Analytical method to apply
Frequency of things in a group		Mode
Measurements on a ranked scale		Median
Measurements on a linear scale		Mean
Visual inspection of chaotic, random, or uncategorized data		None

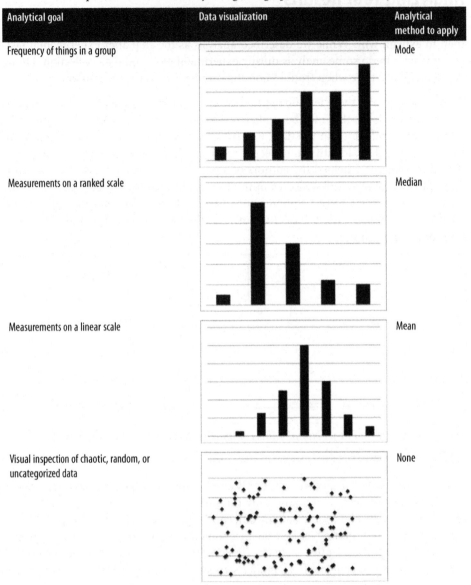

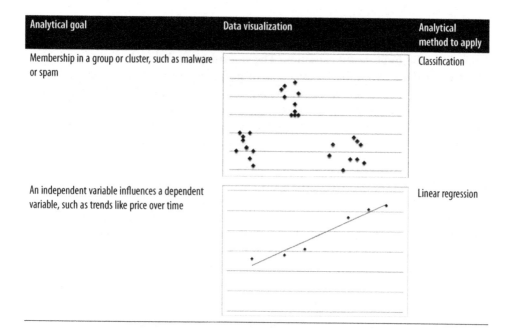

Analytical goal	Data visualization	Analytical method to apply
Membership in a group or cluster, such as malware or spam		Classification
An independent variable influences a dependent variable, such as trends like price over time		Linear regression

One other note about statistics. A statistically significant relationship between two variables is determined from a value called the *chi-squared statistic*. This chi-squared statistic is a number that quantifies the amount of disparity between the actual observed values and the values that would be expected if there were no relationship in the population. The relationship between two variables is considered statistically significant if its probability of occurring is large enough to rule out it occurring by chance. A *p*-value is a probability that measures how likely it is to observe the relationship if there's really no relationship in the population. It is generally accepted that if the *p*-value is less than or equal to .05, you can conclude that there is a statistically significant relationship between the variables.

Outside of formal statistical modeling is a method known as *exploratory data analysis*, which is often used as a first look at experimental data. It has been described as finding the "attitude" of the data, applied before choosing a probabilistic model. Used during or soon after data collection, exploratory data analysis is a cursory look that can reveal mistakes, relationships between variables, and the selection of an analytical method. It is very common to use graphical techniques to explore the data, such as histograms and scatterplots. Remember, however, that as mathematician John Tukey wrote in *Exploratory Data Analysis*, "exploratory data analysis can never be the whole story."

Many people are familiar with the adage "correlation does not imply causation." This error in logic is easy to make if you assume that one event depends (causation) on another for the two to be related (correlation). Correlated events offer scientists valuable insights about things to investigate. However, the legitimate scientist must work to show the cause. Controlled studies can be used to increase confidence that a correlation is a valid indicator of causation. The control group helps show that there is no effect when there *should* be no effect, as in people who receive a placebo in a drug trial. Say you develop a web browser plug-in that warns people of dangerous web pages. There might be a correlation between how many people use the plug-in and the number of dangerous sites they visit, but you should also measure how many dangerous sites a control group—one without your security plug-in—also visits.

To determine causation, first be sure that the effect happened after the cause (see Figure 2-2). In an experiment to study the effects of fatigue on 10-hour shifts in a network operations center, researchers find that people who are tired make more mistakes. Those researchers should have looked to be sure that mistakes happened *after* people were tired. You should also be aware that it can be difficult to identify and rule out other variables. In a 2010 study about victims of phishing attacks, the research results suggested that women and participants between ages 18–25 were more susceptible.[2] They point out, however, that there were limitations to the study, including the fact that participants might have been riskier in the study than in real life.

Figure 2-2. XKCD (http://xkcd.com/552/) comic on correlation

I will introduce a variety of methodologies and considerations for scientific experimentation and analysis in subsequent chapters of this book. If you wish to skip to any in particular, they can be found as shown in Table 2-3.

Table 2-3. Book chapters for experimentation and analysis topics

Experimentation/analysis topic	Chapter
Fuzzing	Chapter 4
False Positive and False Negatives	Chapter 5
Machine Learning	Chapter 6
Security Assumptions and Adversarial Models	Chapter 7

---

2 Who Falls for Phish? A Demographic Analysis of Phishing Susceptibility and Effectiveness of Interventions. (*http://lorrie.cranor.org/pubs/pap1162-sheng.pdf*)

Experimentation/analysis topic	Chapter
Reproducibility and Repeatability	Chapter 8
Game Theory	Chapter 9
Regression	Chapter 10
Double-Blind Experimentation	Chapter 11
Evaluating Visualizations	Chapter 12

Putting Results to Work

After experimentation and analysis, you will often have useful new knowledge, information, or insights. The most obvious way to apply the knowledge gained from science is to improve the use of tools and improve the tools themselves. Take forensics, for example. Your job is forensic analysis and you found a new open source forensic tool. You designed a scientific evaluation and ran a quick experiment to see which tool performs some forensic function faster or more accurately. Now with the knowledge you've gained, you have empirical data about which tool is better for your job.

Sharing your results is an important part of science. Sure, you may have selfish intentions to improve your proprietary product, or you might want to file for a patent. Contributing your results to the public domain does not mean you won't be rewarded. Google's papers on the Google File System, MapReduce, and BigTable opened up whole new fields of development, but they did not inhibit Google's success.

Another way to put your experiment to work is to share the code and data you used. This used to be very rare in computer science, but there is a growing movement toward openness.[3] The common repositories for source code are SourceForge and GitHub. There are two common complaints against publishing code. The first concern is that it's too much work to clean up unpolished or buggy code, and that other users will demand support and bug fixes. I recommend spending a modest amount of time to offer reasonably understandable and useful code, and then making it public as is. The second concern is that your code is proprietary intellectual property. This may be true, but the default decision should be to share, even if it's only code snippets rather than the whole program.

There are lots of ways to share your work and results. Here are some common options, in order of increasing formality:

---

3 In 2013, the White House issued a memo (*http://1.usa.gov/1WtXvWn*) directing public access to research funded by the federal government. In 2014, the National Science Foundation, the funding source for a large portion of federal science and engineering research, launched its own initiative for public access to data (*http://1.usa.gov/1WtXz8y*).

Blogs

Blogs offer an easy way to quickly share results with a broad online audience. Individuals and companies are using this approach. See, for example, Light Blue Touchpaper (*https://www.lightbluetouchpaper.org*), Dell SecureWorks (*http://bit.ly/1WtXPo8*), Synack (*http://bit.ly/1WtXQZf*), and Brian Krebs (*http://bit.ly/1WtXRMK*).

Magazines

Magazines offer an opportunity to publish professionally without the formal process of an academic journal. Examples include *SC Magazine* and *Security Magazine*. *IEEE Security and Privacy Magazine* is a highly respected publication for cybersecurity research but has a more substantial review and editing process.

Conferences

Presenting at a conference is an opportunity to share your work, get feedback from an audience, and build a reputation. The list of conferences is extensive, and each offers a different kind of audience. Some conferences receive a lot of submissions and only accept a select few. There are a few workshops devoted to cybersecurity science, including the LASER Workshop (Learning from Authoritative Security Experiment Results), Workshop on Cyber Security Experimentation and Test (CSET), and Symposium on the Science of Security (HotSoS). For general cybersecurity research conferences, consider the ACM SIGSAC Conference on Computer and Communications Security (CCS), Black Hat, IEEE Symposium on Security and Privacy, and RSA Security Conferences. So-called hacker conferences, such as BSides, CanSecWest, DEF CON, and ShmooCon, offer an informal venue to present security work and results.

Journals

Scientific cybersecurity journals are considered the most respected place to publish research results. Journal articles have conventions for content and format: an introduction and subject-matter background, methodology, results, related work, and conclusions. Unfortunately, the acceptance rates are often low, and the time between submission and publication can be many months. Respected journals include *Computers & Security* and *IEEE Transactions on Information Forensics and Security*.

A Checklist for Conducting Experimentation

Below is a general list of considerations for conducting scientific experimentation in cybersecurity. It captures the major components of the scientific method, and other important considerations and waypoints. Science is too broad to have a universal and concrete, one-size-fits-all checklist and your experiment will almost certainly have modified or expanded steps, but this serves to guide you and help ensure that the important aspects aren't overlooked.

1. Formulate a question to study, the purpose for doing experimentation.
2. Ensure that the topic is nontrivial and important to solve.
3. Conduct a literature review and background research to see what is already known about the topic.
4. Form your hypothesis, ensuring that the statement is testable, reproducible, and falsifiable with an independent and dependent variable.
5. Make some predictions about your hypothesis.
6. Assemble a team to help execute the experiment, if necessary.
7. If studying human subjects, seek institutional review board (IRB) approval.
8. Test your hypothesis. Collect data.
   a. Make a list of data, equipment, and materials you will need.
   b. Carefully determine the procedure you will use to conduct the experiments.
   c. Identify the environment or test facility where you will conduct experimentation (e.g., laboratory, cloud, real world).
   d. Determine the scientific and study instruments you will use (e.g., packet analyzer, oscilloscope, human survey).
   e. Identify necessary sample size to have statistical power.
   f. Conduct your experiments.
      i. Change only one variable at a time to ensure a fair test.
      ii. Record data and observations.
      iii. Sanity check the data during collection to be sure data collection is working properly.
9. Analyze and interpret your data and test results to determine whether you should accept your hypothesis.
10. Check for experimental errors and outliers. Are the results reasonable?
11. Document your experiment.
    a. Include a description of your procedures with enough detail for others to reproduce.
    b. Include details of the data, equipment, configurations, and other materials used in the experiment.
    c. Describe the analytical technique(s) you applied and their results.
    d. Explain your conclusions, including why you did or did not accept your hypothesis.
    e. Honestly explain limitations of your data, approach, and conclusions.

f. Provide considerations for future experiments or impact of your results.

12. Determine if you should modify your hypothesis and conduct further experimentation.

13. Put your results to work by publishing a paper, creating a product, or making a recommendation.

14. Make code and data used in experimentation publicly accessible if possible.

Project Management

Project management for your experiments can be very important, especially for large and complex projects. The scientific method in all projects benefits from careful documentation and record keeping. Something as simple as a notebook might work fine for you.

 For an example of extreme project management, see the 89-page document (*http://bit.ly/1WtY82e*) describing requirements for human life scientific experiments on the International Space Station.

Large projects are likely to have multiple people, schedules, and deadlines—even multiple budgets. Project management for a modest digital forensics experiment involving two or three people might involve multiple code reviews, and weekly meetings to track progress and review of test results. Larger projects often involve collaboration across departments, institutions, or countries and can become unwieldy without disciplined project management.

There are plenty of options for managing projects, communication, development, and documentation. Wikis offer basic collaboration and can be set up with minimal effort and cost. Web-based tools specifically tailored for project management include Basecamp, Redmine, Trello, and Wrike.

Conclusion

This chapter discussed the execution of the scientific method and key points in designing an experiment. The key takeaways are:

- A hypothesis is a testable statement you believe to be true.

- In a fair test, only one experimental variable changes at a time and all other conditions remain the same.

- Analysis helps you determine whether to accept or reject a hypothesis. Statistics is commonly used for analysis, and sample size determines statistical power.

- You can put scientific results to work by building tools and sharing results in blogs, conferences, and journals.

- The checklist in this chapter can help ensure that you've thought about important components of the scientific method.

References

- Matt Bishop. *Computer Security: Art and Science* (Boston, MA: Addison-Wesley Professional, 2002)

- David Freedman, Robert Pisani, Roger Purves. *Statistics, 4th Edition* (New York, NY: W. W. Norton & Company, 2007)

- Learning from Authoritative Security Experiment Results (LASER) Workshops (*http://www.laser-workshop.org*)

- Dahlia K. Remler and Gregg G. Van Ryzin. *Research Methods in Practice* (Thousand Oaks, CA: SAGE Publications, Inc., 2010)

- David Salsburg. *The Lady Tasting Tea: How Statistics Revolutionized Science in the Twentieth Century* (New York, NY: Holt Paperbacks, 2002)

- Dennis Shasha and Cathy Lazere. *Out of Their Minds: The Lives and Discoveries of 15 Great Computer Scientists* (New York, NY: Copernicus, 1998)

- Symposium and Bootcamp on the Science of Security (HotSoS) (*http://hotsos.org*)

- John W. Tukey. *Exploratory Data Analysis* (Reading, MA: Addison-Wesley, 1977)

## CHAPTER 3

Cybersecurity Experimentation and Test Environments

Scientific inquiry and experimentation require time, space, and materials. Depending on type, scale, cost, and other factors, you may want to run an experiment on your laptop, in a lab, on a cloud, or in the real world. In the checklist for experimentation in Chapter 2, an early step in testing a hypothesis was to "identify the environment or test facility where you will conduct experimentation." This chapter explores that topic and explains the trade-offs and choices for different types of experimentation.

One way to think about experimentation is in an ecosystem, in other words, the "living" environment and digital organisms. The most obvious ecosystem is the real world. Knowledge about cybersecurity science is certainly gained by observing and interacting with the real world, and some scientists firmly believe that experimentation should start with the real world because it grounds science in reality.

Sometimes the real world is inappropriate or otherwise undesirable for testing and evaluation. It would be unethical, dangerous, and probably illegal to study the effects of malware by releasing it onto the Internet. It is also challenging to observe or measure real-world systems without affecting them. This phenomenon is called the *observer effect*. Studying the way that users make decisions about cybersecurity choices is valuable, but once subjects know that a researcher is observing them, their behavior changes.

Consider a noncyber analogy. When scientists want to learn about monkeys, sometimes the scientists go into the jungle and observe the monkeys in the wild. The advantage is an opportunity to learn about the monkeys in an undisturbed, natural habitat. Disadvantages include the cost and inconvenience of going into the jungle, and the inability to control all aspects of the experiment. Scientists also learn about monkeys in zoos. A zoo provides more structure and control over the environment while allowing the animals some freedom to exert their natural behavior. Finally, scientists learn about monkeys in cages. This is a highly restrictive ecosystem that enables the scientist to closely monitor and control many variables but greatly inhibits the free and natural behavior of the animal. Each environment is useful for different purposes.

Scientists use the term *ecological validity* to indicate how well a study approximates the real world. In a study of passwords generated by participants for fictitious accounts versus their real passwords, the experimenters said "this is the first study concerning the ecological validity of password creation in user studies...." In many cases, and especially in practical cybersecurity, test environments that reflect the production environment are preferred because you want the test results to mimic performance of the same solution in the wild. Unfortunately, there is no standard measurement or test for ecological validity. It is the experimenter's duty to address challenges to validity.

This chapter will look at environments and test facilities for cybersecurity experimentation. The first section introduces modeling and simulation, one way to test hypotheses offline. Then we'll look at desktop, cloud, and testbed options that offer choices in cost and scale. Finally, we'll discuss datasets that you can use for testing. Keep in mind that there may be no single right answer for how to conduct your tests and experiments. In fact, you might choose to use more than one. People who study botnet behavior, for example, often start with a simulation, then run a controlled test on a small network, and compare these results to real-world data.

Modeling and Simulation

Modeling and simulation are methods of scientific exploration that are carried out in artificial environments. For the results to be useful in the real world, these techniques require informed design and clear statement of assumptions, configurations, and implementations. Modeling and simulation are especially useful in exploring large-scale systems, complex systems, and new conceptual designs. For example, they might be used to investigate an Internet of the future, or how malware spreads on an Internet scale. Questions such as these might only be answered by modeling and simulation, especially if an emergent behavior is not apparent until the experimental scale is large enough.

While "modeling and simulation" are often used together as a single discipline, they are individual concepts. Modeling is the creation of a conceptual object that can predict the behavior of real systems under a set of assumptions and conditions. For example, you could create a model to describe how smartphones move around inside a city. Simulation is the process of applying the model to a particular use case in order to predict the system's behavior. The smartphone simulation could involve approximating an average workday by moving 100,000 hypothetical smartphones around a city of a certain size.

Modeling and simulation can be done in small environments (like on your laptop) and large environments (like supercomputers). Software like MATLAB and R can run many kinds of prebuilt simulations, and contain powerful programming languages with flexibility for new experiments. Simulations can be written in traditional programming languages, using special libraries devoted to those tasks. Some modeling and simulation tools are tailored for specific purposes. For example, ns-3 (*https://www.nsnam.org*) is an open source simulation environment for networking research. Figure 3-1 shows a basic wireless topology that can be created in ns-3 for a functional network simulation; it follows one online tutorial (*https://www.nsnam.org/docs/tutorial/*).

```
// Default Network Topology
//
//    Wifi 10.1.3.0
//                  AP
// *    *    *     *
// |    |    |     |    10.1.1.0
// n5   n6   n7    n0 --------------- n1   n2   n3   n4
//                    point-to-point  |    |    |    |
//                                    ================
//                                    LAN 10.1.2.0
```

Figure 3-1. A simulated wireless network topology in ns-3

The usefulness of modeling and simulation is primarily limited by the ability to define and create a realistic model. Figuring out how to model network traffic, system performance, user behavior, and any other relevant variables is a challenging task. Within the cybersecurity community there remain unsolved questions about how to quantify and measure whether an experiment is realistic enough.

Simulating human behavior is strongly desirable in simulations. A simulated network without any simulated user traffic or activity limits its value, and can make the simulation ineffective. It can be useful to simulate normal activity in some scenarios, and malicious or anomalous activity in other experiments. One solution is to replay previously recorded traffic from real users or networks. This requires access to such datasets and limits your control over the type and tempo of activity. Another solution is to use customizable software agents. Note that these agents are more advanced than network traffic generators because they attempt to simulate real human behavior. Examples of software agents include NCRBot, built for the National Cyber Range, and SIMPass, specifically designed to simulate human password behavior. DASH is an agent-based platform for simulating human behavior that was designed specifically for the DETER Testbed (see Table 3-4).

Open Datasets for Testing

Publicly available datasets are good for science. A *dataset*, or corpus, allows research-ers to reproduce experiments and compare the implementation and performance of tools using the same data. Public datasets also save you from having to find relevant and representative data, or worry about getting permission to use private or propriet-ary data. The Enron Corpus is one example of a public dataset, and contains over 600,000 real emails from the collapsed Enron Corporation. This collection has been a valuable source of data for building and testing cybersecurity solutions. Additional datasets are listed in Table 3-1.

The primary challenges with creating open datasets are realism and privacy. The community has not yet discovered how to create sufficiently realistic artificial laboratory-created cyber data.

 Data from real, live networks and the Internet often contains sensi-tive and personal information, sensitive company details, or could reveal security vulnerabilities of the data provider if publicly dis-tributed. Anonymization of IP addresses and personally identifia-ble information is one way to sanitize live data. Another is to restrict a dataset to particular uses or users.

Table 3-1. Datasets available for cybersecurity science

Dataset	Description
MIT Lincoln Laboratory IDS Datasets (*http://www.ll.mit.edu/ideval/data*)	Examples of background and attacks traffic
NSA Cyber Defense Exercise Dataset (*http://www.usma.edu/crc/SitePages/DataSets.aspx*)	Snort, DNS, web server, and Splunk logs
Internet-Wide Scan Data Repository (*https://scans.io*)	Large collection of Internet-wide scanning data from Rapid7, the University of Michigan, and others
Center for Applied Internet Data Analysis (CAIDA) Datasets (*http://imdc.datcat.org*)	Internet measurement with collaboration of numerous institutions, academics, commercial and noncommercial contributors, including anonymized Internet traces, Code Red worm propagation, passive traces on high-speed links
Protected Repository for the Defense of Infrastructure Against Cyber Threats (PREDICT) (*https://www.predict.org*)	Several levels of data datasets (unrestricted, quasi-restricted, and restricted), including BGP routing data, blackhole data, IDS and firewall data, and unsolicited bulk email data
Amazon Web Services Datasets (*http://aws.amazon.com/public-data-sets/*)	Public datasets that can easily be attached to Amazon cloud-based applications, including the Enron Corpus (email), Common Crawl corpus (millions of crawled web pages), and geographical data

Because cybersecurity is inherently about human communication, datasets might be protected as human subjects research (HSR). When human beings are the research subjects, various institutional and corporate policies help ensure that the humans are appropriately protected.

Desktop Testing

Desktop testing is perhaps the most common environment for cybersecurity science. Commodity laptops and workstations often provide sufficient computing resources for developers, administrators, and scientists to run scientific experiments. Using one's own computer is also convenient and cost-effective. Desktop virtualization solutions such as QEMU, VirtualBox, and VMware Workstation are widespread and offer the additional benefits of snapshots and revertible virtual machines.

DARPA has built and released an open source operating system extension to Linux called DECREE (DARPA Experimental Cybersecurity Research Evaluation Environment) that is tailored especially for computer security research and experimentation. The platform is intentionally simple (just seven system calls), safe (custom executable format), and reproducible (from the kernel up). DECREE is available on GitHub (*https://github.com/CyberGrandChallenge*) as a Vagrant box and also works in VirtualBox and VMware.

Scientific tests do not inherently require specialized hardware or software. Depending on what you are studying, common desktop applications such as Microsoft Excel can be used to analyze data. In other cases, it is convenient or necessary to use benchmarking or analysis software to collect performance metrics. Many users prefer virtualization to compartmentalize their experiments or to create a virtual machine preloaded with useful tools. Table 3-2 is a brief list of free and open source software that could be used for a science-oriented cybersecurity workstation.

Table 3-2. Free and open source software that may be useful for cybersecurity science

Software	Function
R	Statistical computing and graphics
gnuplot	Function and data plotting
Latex	Document preparation
Scilab	Numerical computation
SciPy	Python packages for mathematics, science, and engineering
iPython	Shell for interactive computing
Pandas	Python data manipulation and analysis library
KVM and QEMU	Virtualization
Wireshark	Network traffic capture and analysis

Software	Function
ns-3	Modeling and simulation
Scapy	Packet manipulation
gcc	GNU compiler collection
binutils	GNU binary utilities
Valgrind	Instrumentation framework for dynamic analysis
iperf	TCP/UDP bandwidth measurement
netperf	Network performance benchmark
RAMspeed	Cache and memory benchmark
IOzone	Filesystem benchmark
LMbench	Performance analysis
Peach Fuzzer	Fuzzing platform

Desktop testing is mostly limited by the resources of the machine, including memory, CPU, storage, and network speed. Comparing the performance and correctness of one encryption algorithm against another can be done with desktop-quality resources. An average workstation running ns-3 can easily handle thousands of simulated hosts. However, the US Army Research Laboratory ran an ns-3 scaling experiment in 2012 and achieved 360,448,000 simulated nodes using 176 servers. Malware analysis, forensics, software fuzzing, and many other scientific questions can be explored on your desktop, and they can produce significant and meaningful scientific results.

Cloud Computing

If a desktop environment is too limiting for your experiment, cloud computing is another option. Cloud computing offers one key set of advantages: cost and scale. Inherent in the definition of cloud computing is metered service, paying only for what you use. For experimentation, this is almost always cheaper than buying the same number of servers on-site. Given the seemingly "unlimited" resources of major cloud providers, you also benefit from very large-scale environments that are impractical and cost-prohibitive on-site. Compared with desktop testing, which is slow with limited resources, you can quickly provision a temporary cloud machine—or cluster of machines—with very large CPU, memory, or networking resources. In cases where your work can be parallelized, the cloud architecture can also help get your work done faster. Password cracking is commonly used as an example of an embarrassingly parallel workload, and cloud-based password cracking has garnered much media attention.

Cloud environments provide several scientifically relevant attributes. First, reproducibility is enhanced because you can precisely describe the environment used for a test. With Amazon Web Services, for example, virtual machines have a unique identifier

(AMI) that you can reference. To document the hardware and software setup for your experiment, you might say, "I used ami-a0c7a6c8 running on an m1.large instance." Microsoft, Rackspace, and other cloud providers have similar constructs, as shown in Table 3-3.

Table 3-3. Several cloud providers that offer services for cybersecurity science

Cloud provider	Description
Amazon Web Services (*http://aws.amazon.com*)	One of the largest and most widely used cloud providers, including a free tier
PlanetLab (*https://www.planet-lab.org*)	Publicly available cloud-based global testbed aimed at network and distributed systems research
CloudLab (*http://www.cloudlab.us*)	A "scientific instrument" with instrumentation and transparency to see how the system is operating, and the ability to publish hardware and software profiles for external repeatability

Many companies, universities, and organizations now have their own on-premise cloud or cloudlike solution for internal use. This environment combines the attributes and benefits of cloud computing with increased security, local administration, and support. You may benefit from this kind of shared resource for conducting tests and experiments.

Cybersecurity Testbeds

Cybersecurity testbeds, sometimes called *ranges*, have emerged in the past decade to provide shared resources devoted to furthering cybersecurity research and experimentation. Testbeds can include physical and/or virtual components, and may be general purpose or highly specialized for a specific focus area. In addition to the collection of hardware and software, most testbeds include support tools: testbed control and provisioning, network or user emulators, instrumentation for data collection and situational awareness. Table 3-4 lists some testbeds applicable to cybersecurity. While some testbeds are completely open to the public, many are restricted to academia or other limited communities. Every year, new testbeds and testbed research appears at research workshops such as CSET and LASER.

For those committed to scientific experimentation in the long term, investing in public or private testbed infrastructure is advantageous. Your cybersecurity testbed could be dual-purposed for nonscientific business processes as well, including training, quality assurance, or testing and evaluation (see Table 3-4). Experiment facilities with limited capacity or capabilities can unfortunately limit the research questions that a researcher wishes to explore. Therefore, carefully consider what you will invest in before committing.

Table 3-4. Testbeds for cybersecurity

Testbed	Focus area
Anubis (*https://anubis.iseclab.org*)	Malware analysis
Connected Vehicle Testbed (*http://www.its.dot.gov/testbed.htm*)	Connected vehicles
DETER (*http://deter-project.org*)	Cybersecurity experimentation and testing
DRAKVUF (*http://drakvuf.com*)	Virtualized, desktop dynamic malware analysis
EDURange (*http://edurange.org*)	Training and exercises
Emulab (*http://www.emulab.net*)	Network testbed
Future Internet of Things (FIT) Lab (*https://www.iot-lab.info*)	Wireless sensors and Internet of Things
Future Internet Research & Experimentation (FIRE) (*http://www.ict-fire.eu*)	European federation of testbeds
GENI (Global Environment for Network Innovations) (*http://www.geni.net*)	Networking and distributed systems
NITOS (Network Implementation Testbed using Open Source) (*http://nitlab.inf.uth.gr*)	Wireless
OFELIA (OpenFlow in Europe: Linking Infrastructure and Applications) (*http://www.fp7-ofelia.eu*)	OpenFlow software-defined networking
ORBIT (Open-Access Research Testbed for Next-Generation Wireless Networks) (*http://www.orbit-lab.org*)	Wireless
PlanetLab (*https://www.planet-lab.org*)	Global-scale network research
StarBed (*http://starbed.nict.go.jp/en/*)	Internet simulations

One testbed that you might not immediately think of is a human testbed. It can be tricky to find environments with a large number of voluntary human subjects willing to participate in your study or experiment. Amazon Mechanical Turk (*https://www.mturk.com*) was designed as a marketplace for crowdsourced human work, where volunteers are paid small amounts for completing tasks. Researchers have found that results from Mechanical Turk are scientifically valid and can rapidly produce inexpensive high-quality data.

A Checklist for Selecting an Experimentation and Test Environment

Here is a 10-point checklist to use when deciding on an experimentation or test environment:

1. Identify the technical requirements for your test or experiment.
2. Establish what testbed(s) you may have access to based on your affiliation (e.g., business sector, public, academic, etc.).
3. Estimate how much money you want to spend.
4. Decide how much control and flexibility you want over the environment.

5. Determine how much realism, fidelity, and ecological validity you need in the environment.

6. Establish how much time, expertise, and desire you have to spend configuring the test environment.

7. Calculate the scale/size you plan the experiment to be.

8. Consider whether a domain-specific testbed (e.g., malware, wireless, etc.) is appropriate.

9. Identify the dataset that you will use, if required.

10. Create a plan to document and describe the environment to others in a repeatable way.

Conclusion

This chapter described important considerations for choosing the environment or test facility for experimentation. The key takeaways were:

- Cybersecurity experiments vary in their ecological validity, which is how well they approximate the real world.

- Modeling and simulation are useful in exploring large-scale systems, complex systems, and new conceptual designs. Modeling and simulation are primarily limited by the ability to define and create a realistic model.

- There are a variety of open datasets available for tool testing and scientific experimentation. Public datasets allow researchers to reproduce experiments and compare tools using common data.

- Cybersecurity experimentation can be done on desktop computers, cloud computing environments, and cybersecurity testbeds. Each brings a different amount of computational resources and cost.

References

- David Balenson, Laura Tinnel, and Terry Benzel. *Cybersecurity Experimentation of the Future (CEF): Catalyzing a New Generation of Experimental Cybersecurity Research (http://www.cyberexperimentation.org/report/).*

- Michael Gregg. *The Network Security Test Lab* (Indianapolis, IN: Wiley, 2015)

- Mohammad S. Obaidat, Faouzi Zarai, and Petros Nicopolitidis (eds.). *Modeling and Simulation of Computer Networks and Systems* (Waltham, MA: Morgan Kaufmann, 2015)

- William R. Shadish, Thomas D. Cook, and Donald T. Campbell. *(2002) Experimental and Quasi-experimental Designs for Generalized Causal Inference* (Boston, MA: Houghton Mifflin, 2002)

- Angela B. Shiflet and George W. Shiflet. *Introduction to Computational Science: Modeling and Simulation for the Sciences (Second Edition)* (Princeton, NJ: Princeton University Press, 2014)

- USENIX Workshops on Cyber Security Experimentation and Test (CSET) (*https://www.usenix.org/conferences/byname/135*)

## CHAPTER 4

Software Assurance

Software assurance, an important subdiscipline of software engineering, is the confidence that software will run as expected and be free of vulnerabilities. Given the weight and importance of these tasks, scientific experimentation and evaluation can help ensure that software is secure. In this chapter, we will look at the intersection of software assurance and cybersecurity science. We will use fuzzing as an example of experimentally testing a hypothesis, the importance and design of an adversarial model, and how to put the scientific method to work in evaluating software exploitability.

The Department of Homeland Security describes software assurance as "trustworthiness, predictable execution, and conformance." Programmers and cybersecurity practitioners spend a lot of time finding and mitigating vulnerabilities to build software assurance, and cybersecurity science can aid that practice. "Since software engineering is in its adolescence, it is certainly a candidate for the experimental method of analysis. Experimentation is performed in order to help us better evaluate, predict, understand, control, and improve the software development process and product." This quote is from an article from 1986, and is as true today as it was then.

In an ideal world, software developers could apply a magic process to confirm without a doubt that software is secure. Unfortunately, such a solution is not available, or at least not easily and universally available for all software. Formal verification uses the field of formal methods in mathematics to prove the correctness of algorithms, protocols, circuits, and other systems. The Common Criteria, and before it the Trusted Computer System Evaluation Criteria, provides standards for computer security certification. Documentation, analysis, and testing determine the evaluation assurance level (EAL) of a system. FreeBSD and Windows 7, for example, have both obtained EAL Level 4 ("Methodically Designed, Tested, and Reviewed").

There are plenty of interesting scientific experiments in software assurance. For example, if you want to know how robust your company's new music streaming service is, you could design the experiment methodology to test the software in a large-scale environment that simulates thousands of real-world users. Perhaps you want to know how to deploy or collect telemetry—automatic, remote collection of metrics and measurements—from Internet-connected vehicles, and need to find the balance of frequent transmissions of real-time data versus the cost of data connectivity. Software assurance is especially sensitive to correctly modeling the threat, so you might experiment with the realism of the test conditions themselves. Discovering new ways to automate the instrumentation and testing of software will continue to be valuable to software assurance.

An Example Scientific Experiment in Software Assurance

A fundamental research question in software assurance is "how do we find all the unknown vulnerabilities in a piece of software?" This question arises from the practical desire to create secure solutions, especially as software grows ever larger and complex.[1] A few general techniques have emerged in the past decade that practitioners rely on to find vulnerabilities. Some techniques are tailored for specific situations, such as static analysis when source code is available. Others can be applied in a variety of situations. Here are some of the more common software assurance techniques:

Static analysis
Looks for vulnerabilities without executing the program. This may include source code analysis, if available.

Dynamic analysis
Runs the program looking for anomalies or vulnerabilities based on different program inputs. Often done in instrumented sandbox environments.

Fuzzing
A specific type of dynamic analysis in which many pseudorandom inputs are provided to the program to find vulnerabilities.

Penetration testing
The manual or automated search for vulnerabilities by attempting to exploit system vulnerabilities and misconfigurations, often including human users.

For an example of scientific experimentation in software assurance, look at the paper "Optimizing Seed Selection for Fuzzing" (*https://www.usenix.org/system/files/confer ence/usenixsecurity14/sec14-paper-rebert.pdf*) by Rebert et al. (2014). Because it is

---

[1] Firefox has 12 million source lines of code (SLOC) and Chrome has 17 million as of June 2015 (*https:// www.openhub.net*). Windows 8 is rumored to be somewhere between 30 million and 80 million SLOC.

computationally prohibitive to feed every possible input to a program you are analyzing, such as a PDF reader, the experimenter must choose the least number of inputs or seeds to find the most bugs in the target program. The following abstract describes the experiment and results of this experiment. The implied hypothesis is that the quality of seed selection can maximize the total number of bugs found during a fuzz campaign.

Abstract from a software assurance experiment

Randomly mutating well-formed program inputs or simply fuzzing, is a highly effective and widely used strategy to find bugs in software. Other than showing fuzzers find bugs, there has been little systematic effort in understanding the science of how to fuzz properly. In this paper, we focus on how to mathematically formulate and reason about one critical aspect in fuzzing: how best to pick seed files to maximize the total number of bugs found during a fuzz campaign. We design and evaluate six different algorithms using over 650 CPU days on Amazon Elastic Compute Cloud (EC2) to provide ground truth data. Overall, we find 240 bugs in 8 applications and show that the choice of algorithm can greatly increase the number of bugs found. We also show that current seed selection strategies as found in Peach may fare no better than picking seeds at random. We make our data set and code publicly available.

Consider some ways that you could build and extend on this result. Software assurance offers some interesting opportunities for cross-disciplinary scientific exploration. Think of questions that bridge the cyber aspect with a non-cyber aspect, such as economics or psychology. Could you use the fuzzing experiment as a way to measure questions like: Does your company produce more secure software if a new developer is paired with an experienced employee to instill a culture of security awareness? Do developers who are risk-averse in the physical world produce more security-conscious choices in the software they create? Multi-disciplinary research can be a rich and interesting source of scientific questioning.

Fuzzing for Software Assurance

Fuzzing is one method for experimentally testing a hypothesis in the scientific method. For example, a hypothesis might be that *my webapp can withstand 10,000 examples of malformed input without crashing*. Fuzzing has been around since the 1980s and offers an automated, scalable approach to testing how software handles various input. In 2007, Microsoft posted on its blog (*http://blogs.microsoft.com/cyber trust/2007/09/20/fuzz-testing-at-microsoft-and-the-triage-process/*) that it uses fuzz testing internally to test and analyze its own software, saying "it does happen to be one of our most scalable testing approaches to detecting program failures that may have security implications."

Choosing fuzzing for your experimental methodology is only the start. Presumably you have already narrowed your focus to a particular aspect of the software attack surface. You must also make some assumptions about your adversaries, a topic we will cover later in this chapter. It usually makes sense to use a model-based fuzzer that understands the protocols and input formats. If you are fuzzing XML input, then you can generate test cases for every valid field plus try breaking all the rules. In the interest of repeatability, you must track which test case triggers a given failure. Finally, you certainly want to fuzz the software in as realistic an environment as possible. Use production-quality code in the same configuration and environment as it will be deployed.

Fuzzing requires some decisions that impact the process. For example, if the fuzzer is generating random data, you must decide when to stop fuzzing. Previous scientific exploration has helped uncover techniques for correlating fuzzing progress based on code coverage, but code coverage may not be your goal. Even if you run a fixed number of test cases, what does it mean if no crashes or bugs are found? There is also a fundamental challenge in monitoring the target application to know if and why a fuzzed input affected the target application. Furthermore, generating crashes is much easier than tracking down the software bug that caused the crash.

Fuzzing may seem like a random and chaotic process that doesn't belong in the scientific method. Admittedly, this can be true if used carelessly, but that holds for *any* experimental method. Scientific rigor can improve the validity of information you get from fuzzing. The reason behind why you choose fuzzing over any other technique is also important. A user who applies fuzzing to blindly find crashes is accomplishing a valuable task, but that alone is not a scientific task. Fuzzing must help test a hypothesis, and must adhere to the scientific principles previously discussed in "The Scientific Method" on page 7, including repeatability and reproducibility.

At the opposite end of the bug-finding spectrum from fuzzing are formal methods. Formal methods can be used to evaluate a hypothesis using mathematical models for verifying complex hardware and software systems. SLAM (*http://research.micro soft.com/en-us/projects/slam/*), a Microsoft Research project, is such a software model checker. The SLAM engine can be used to check if Windows device drivers satisfy driver API usage rules, for example. Formal methods are best suited for situations where source code is available.

Recall from Chapter 1 that empirical methods are based on observations and experience. By contrast, theoretical methods are based on theory or pure logic. Fuzzing is an empirical method of scientific knowledge. Empirical methods don't necessarily have to occur in the wild or by observing the real world. Empirical strategies can also take many forms including exploratory surveys, case studies, and experiments. The way to convert software assurance claims into validated facts is with the experimental scientific method.

The Scientific Method and the Software Development Life Cycle

Software assurance comes from following development best practices, and from consciously, deliberately adding security measures into the process. The software development life cycle (SDLC) is surprisingly similar to the scientific method, as you can see in Figure 4-1. Both processes have an established procedure which helps ensure that the final product or result is of high quality. The IEEE Standard Glossary even says "Software Engineering means application of systematic, disciplined, quantifiable approach to development, operation, and maintenance of software." The adjectives used to describe this approach mirror those of the approach to scientific exploration. However, just because both have a defined structure, simply following the process-oriented SDLC does not necessarily mean you are doing science or following the scientific method.

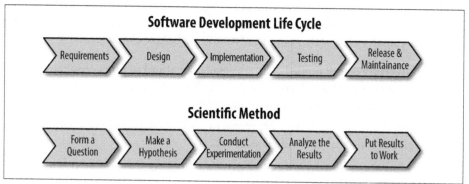

Figure 4-1. Comparison of the software development life cycle with the scientific method

There are opportunities to apply the scientific method in the development life cycle. First, scientific exploration can be applied to the SDLC process itself. For example, do developers find more bugs than dedicated test engineers, or what is the optimal amount of time to spend testing in order to balance security and risk? Second, science can inform or improve specific stages of the SDLC. For example, is pair-programming more efficient or more secure than individual programming, or what is the optimal number of people who should conduct code reviews?

The SDLC also has lessons to teach you about the scientific method. Immersing yourself in the scientific method can sometimes cause you to lose sight of the goal. Science may prove beneficial to cybersecurity practitioners by allowing them to do their jobs better, improving their products, and generating value for their employers. The SDLC helps maximize productivity, and satisfy customer needs and demands, and science for its own sake might not be your goal.

Adversarial Models

Defining a realistic and accurate model of the adversary is an important and complicated undertaking. As we will see in Chapter 7, provable security relies on a model of the system and an attack model. Cybersecurity as applied to software assurance and other domains requires us to consider the motivations, capabilities, and actions of those seeking to compromise the security of a system. This challenge extends to human red teams who may attempt to emulate an adversary and also to algorithms and software emulations of adversaries. Even modeling normal user behavior is challenging because humans rarely act as predictably and routinely as an algorithm. The best network traffic emulators today allow the researcher to define user activity like 70% web traffic (to a defined list of websites) and 30% email traffic (with static or garbage content). Another choice for scientific experimentation (and training) is to use live traffic or captures of real adversary activity.

Sandia National Laboratories' Information Design Assurance Red Team (IDART) has been studying and developing adversary models for some time. For example, it has described a small nation state example adversary with these characteristics:[2]

- The adversary is well funded. The adversary can afford to hire consultants or buy other expertise. This adversary can also buy commercial technology. These adversaries can even afford to develop new or unique attacks.

- This adversary has aggressive programs to acquire education knowledge in technologies that also may provide insider access.

- This adversary will use classic intelligence methods to obtain insider information and access.

- This adversary will learn all design information.

- The adversary is risk averse. It will make every effort to avoid detection.

- This adversary has specific goals for attacking a system.

- This adversary is creative and very clever. It will seek out unconventional methods to achieve its goals.

It is one thing to define these characteristics on paper and quite another to apply them to a real-world security evaluation. This remains an open problem today. What would it look like to test your cyber defenses against a risk-averse adversary? Here might be one way: say you set up a penetration test using Metaploit and Armitage, plus Cortana, the scripting language for Armitage. You could create a script that acts

---

2 B. J. Wood and R. A. Duggan. "Red Teaming of Advanced Information Assurance Concepts," DARPA Information Survivability Conference and Exposition, pp.112-118 vol.2, 2000.

like a risk-averse adversary by, for example, waiting five minutes after seeing a vulnerable machine before attempting to exploit it (Example 4-1).

Example 4-1. A Cortana script that represents a risk-averse adversary

```
#
# This script waits for a box with port 445 open to appear,
# waits 5 minutes, and then
# launches the ms08_067_netapi exploit at it.
#
# A modified version of
# https://github.com/rsmudge/cortana-scripts/blob/master/autohack/autohack.cna
#

# auto exploit any Windows boxes
on service_add_445 {
    sleep(5 * 60 * 1000);
    println("Exploiting $1 (" . host_os($1) . ")");
    if (host_os($1) eq "Microsoft Windows") {
        exploit("windows/smb/ms08_067_netapi", $1);
    }
}

on session_open {
    println("Session $1 opened. I got " . session_host($1) .
        " with " . session_exploit($1));
}
```

The bottom line is that good scientific inquiry considers the assumptions about the capabilities of an adversary, such as what he or she can see or do. Journal papers often devote a section (or subsection) to explaining the adversary model. For example, the authors might state that "we assume a malicious eavesdropper where the eavesdropper can collect WiFi signals in public places." As you create and conduct scientific experiments, remember to define your adversarial model. For additional references and discussions on real-world adversary simulations, see the blog posts from cybersecurity developer Raphael Mudge (*http://blog.cobaltstrike.com/category/adversary-simulation/*).

Case Study: The Risk of Software Exploitability

Software assurance experts sometimes assume that all bugs are created equal. For a complex system such as an operating system, it can be impractical to address every bug and every crash. Software development organizations typically have an issue-tracking system like Jira (*https://www.atlassian.com/software/jira*), which documents bugs and allows the organization to prioritize the order in which issues are addressed.

Not all bugs are created equal. As discussed earlier, risk is a function of threats, vulnerabilities, and impact. Even with a carefully calculated risk analysis, understanding the likelihood or probability of that risk occurring is vital. The Common Vulnerability Scoring System (CVSS) is a standard for measuring vulnerability risk. A CVSS score takes into account various metrics, such as attack vector (network, local, physical), user interaction (required or not required), and exploitability (unproven, proof of concept, functional, high, not defined). Figure 4-2 shows the CVSS information for Heartbleed. Calculating CVSS scores requires a thorough understanding of the vulnerability, and is not easily done for every crash you generate. Microsoft's crash analyzer, !exploitable, also calculates an exploitability rating (exploitable, probably exploitable, probably not exploitable, or unknown), and does so based solely on crash dumps. Microsoft says that the tool can tell you, "This is the sort of crash that experience tells us is likely to be exploitable."

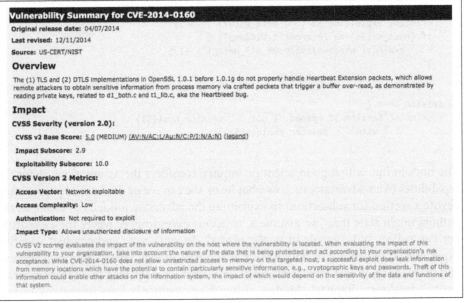

Figure 4-2. National Vulnerability Database entry for Heartbleed (CVE-2014-0160)

A New Experiment

Consider a hypothetical scientific experiment to determine the likelihood of exploitability. Say you are a developer for a new embedded system that runs on an Internet-enabled pedometer. Testing has already revealed a list of crashes and you would like to scientifically determine which bugs to fix first based on their likelihood of exploitability. Fixing bugs results in a better product that will bring your company increased sales and revenue. One question you could consider is how attackers have gone after other embedded systems like yours. Historical and related data can be very insightful.

Unfortunately, it isn't possible to test a hypothesis like "attackers will go after my product in similar ways to Product Y" until your product is actually attacked, at which point you will have data to support the claim. It is also difficult to predict how dedicated adversaries, including researchers, may attack your product. However, it is possible to use fuzzing to generate crashes, and from that information you can draw a hypothesis. Consider this hypothesis:

> Crashes in other similar software can help predict the most frequent crashes in our new code.

The intuition behind this hypothesis is that some crashes are more prevalent than others, that there are identifiable features of these crashes shared between software, and that you can use historical knowledge to identify vulnerable code in new software. It's better to predict frequent crashes than to wait and see what consumers report. You begin by gathering crashes that might indicate bugs in your own product. This list could come from fuzzing, penetration testing, everyday use of the software, or other crash-generating mechanisms. You also need crash information from other similar products, either from your company or competitors. By fuzzing both groups, you can apply some well-known techniques and determine if the hypothesis holds.

Here's one approach:

1. Check for known vulnerabilities in the National Vulnerability Database (*https://nvd.nist.gov*). As of June 2015, there were no entries in the database for Fitbits.

2. Use Galileo (*https://bitbucket.org/benallard/galileo/overview*), a Python utility for communicating with Fitbit devices, to enable fuzzing.

3. Use the Peach fuzzer or a custom Python script, based on the following, to send random data to the device trying to generate crashes:

```
# Connect to the Fitbit USB dongle
device = usb.core.find(idVendor=0x2687, idProduct=0xfb01)

# Send data to the Fitbit tracker (through the dongle)
device.write(endpoint, data, timeout)

# Read responses from the tracker (through the dongle)
response = device.read(endpoint, length, timeout)
```

4. Say you find six inputs that crash the Fitbit. Attach eight attributes to each crash:

- Stack trace
- Size of crashing method (in bytes)
- Size of crashing method (in lines of code)
- Number of parameters to the crashing method
- Number of conditional statements

- Halstead complexity measures
- Cyclomatic complexity
- Nesting-level complexity

5. Apply automatic feature selection in R with Recursive Feature Elimination (RFE) to identify attributes that are (and are not) required to build an accurate model.

```
# Set the seed to ensure the results are repeatable
set.seed(7)

# Load the libraries that provide RFE
library(mlbench)
library(caret)

# Load the data
data(FitbitCrashData)

# Define the control using a random forest selection function
control <- rfeControl(functions=rfFuncs, method="cv", number=10)

# Run the RFE algorithm
results <- rfe(FitbitCrashData[,1:8], FitbitCrashData[,9],
               sizes=c(1:8), rfeControl=control)

# Summarize the results
print(results)

# List the chosen features
predictors(results)

# Plot the results
plot(results, type=c("g", "o"))
```

Without going into depth, *machine learning* is an approach that builds a model from input data and learns how to make predictions without being told explicitly how to do so (machine learning is covered in Chapter 6). This technique is good for testing the hypothesis because we don't know whether crashes in our new code are related to crashes in the other software. Within machine learning is a process called feature selection, which is designed to identify the attributes that most effect the model. For example, a crash feature might be the number of parameters to the code function that crashed. Perhaps crashes are more frequent in functions with more parameters. Feature selection also weeds out irrelevant attributes; maybe the number of lines of code in the crashing function has no statistical correlation with the number of crashes.

For a technical deep dive into this process, see "Which Crashes Should I Fix First?: Predicting Top Crashes at an Early Stage to Prioritize Debugging Efforts" (*http://ieeexplore.ieee.org/xpls/abs_all.jsp?arnumber=5711013*) by Kim et al. (2011).

In the end, you will want to show that machine learning, based on related software crashes, accurately predicted frequent crashes in your new code.

How to Find More Information

Research in many software assurance areas—especially vulnerability discovery—is presented in general cybersecurity journals and conferences but also at domain-specific venues including the International Conference on Software Security and Reliability and the International Symposium on Empirical Software Engineering and Measurement. Popular publications for scientific advances in software assurance are the journal *Empirical Software Engineering* and *IEEE Transactions on Software Engineering*.

Conclusion

This chapter described the intersection of cybersecurity science and software assurance. The key concepts and takeaways are:

- Scientific experimentation and evaluation can help ensure that software is secure.
- Scientists continue to study how to find unknown vulnerabilities in software.
- Fuzzing is one method for experimentally testing a hypothesis in the scientific method.
- The scientific method and the software development life cycle each provide structure and process, but neither replaces the other.
- Realistic and accurate models of adversaries are important to cybersecurity science, and one must consider assumptions about the capabilities of an adversary.

References

- Mark Dowd, John McDonald, Justin Schuh. *The Art of Software Security Assessment: Identifying and Preventing Software Vulnerabilities* (Boston, MA: Addison-Wesley Professional, 2006)
- Gary McGraw. *Software Security: Building Security In* (Boston, MA: Addison-Wesley Professional, 2006)

- Claes Wohlin et al. *Experimentation in Software Engineering* (Heidelberg: Springer, 2012)

## CHAPTER 5

Intrusion Detection and Incident Response

Computer security intrusion detection and incident response began as an academic and scientific study in the 1980s. One of the first intrusion detection papers, written by Dorothy Denning, introduced an anomaly detection model that describes the foundation of the technology even today. "The model is based on the hypothesis that security violations can be detected by monitoring a system's audit records for abnormal patterns of system usage," Denning wrote.[1] Intrusion detection continues to evolve and remains an active area of research and development. The field of incident response emerged from practitioners in response to technology misuse. The first computer emergency response team, the CERT Coordination Center (*http://www.cert.org/about/*), was created in 1988 in response to the Morris worm. The need to respond and manage security incidents is a practical one, but also an area that can be improved through science. In fact, the practice of incident response naturally includes scientific, or at least scientific-like, inquiry to investigate what, how, and why an incident occurred. Rigor in incident response can be especially important if the incident may eventually become part of a legal proceeding.

Rigor isn't just about following a process. Be sure to document what you tried, what worked and didn't work, and gaps you identified. This is important not only for legal matters, but also for developing new hypotheses later.

Scientific work in intrusion detection and incident response today continues to focus on improving the speed and effectiveness of real-world solutions, especially as net-

---

1 Dorothy Denning. "An Intrusion-Detection Model," *IEEE Transactions on Software Engineering*, Volume SE-13, Issue 2, Feb. 1987

work speeds increase. Research and development are also active in applying detection and response to new technologies, from SCADA to the Internet of Things. In recent years the scope of intrusion detection has broadened from a standalone, dedicated IDS machine to distributed, coordinated detection and big data analytics. Scientific thinking can also help dispel intrusion detection folk wisdom like "polymorphic attacks give attackers an advantage" and "antivirus products universally cause a significant performance penalty to workstations."

In this chapter, you'll learn how to scientifically evaluate choices for purchasing an intrusion detection system (IDS), how false positives and false negatives affect scientific analysis, how to measure performance and scalability, and how to conduct an example experiment to maximize Snort IDS signature performance.

An Example Scientific Experiment in Intrusion Detection

For an example of scientifically informed development and evaluation in intrusion detection, look at the paper "A Lone Wolf No More: Supporting Network Intrusion Detection with Real-Time Intelligence" (*http://www.icir.org/johanna/papers/ raid12loneWolf.pdf*) by Amann, Sommer, Sharma, and Hall (2012). In the following abstract, you can see that the implied hypothesis is that integrating external intelligence into the IDS decision process produces a broader view that increases reliability of detecting complex attacks. While the primary goal is developing an enhanced IDS solution, the scientific method is used for performance evaluation to determine volume and latency. The authors test the proposed solution under realistic workloads to measure the traffic volume and added delays introduced by their new feature. Unfortunately, the authors do not measure changes in reliability (other than anecdotal evidence) with which to truly evaluate the hypothesis.

Abstract from an intrusion detection experiment
For network intrusion detection systems it is becoming increasingly difficult to reliably report today's complex attacks without having external context at hand. Unfortunately, however, today's IDS cannot readily integrate intelligence, such as dynamic blacklists, into their operation. In this work, we introduce a fundamentally new capability into IDS processing that vastly broadens a system's view beyond what is visible directly on the wire. We present a novel Input Framework that integrates external information in real-time into the IDS decision process, independent of specific types of data, sources, and desired analyses. We implement our design on top of an open-source IDS, and we report initial experiences from real-world deployment in a large-scale network environment. To ensure that our system meets operational constraints, we further evaluate its technical characteristics in terms of the intelligence volume it can handle under realistic workloads, and the latency with which real-time updates become available to

the IDS analysis engine. The implementation is freely available as open-source software.[2]

Because this implementation is available as open source software, it would be easy to develop a competing implementation and compare the two solutions. Alternatively, you may wish to test this solution in a live network and report on a case study of how well it works in your environment compared to your existing intrusion detection system.

An Unexpected Example of Intrusion Detection

In Neal Stephenson's book *Reamde*, the main character, Richard, takes on an intrusion detection problem: people entering airport terminals by walking upstream through an exit portal and causing a security shutdown. Richard sees guarding against these intruders as an example of a desperately boring job where incidents occur too infrequently (once or twice per year) for guards to remain vigilant.

To test this hypothesis, Richard translates a stream of humans in a hallway into equivalently moving avatars in his massively multiplayer online role-playing game. He offers rewards for players who catch goblins sneaking the wrong way through the passageway. Richard adds fictitious, virtual wrong-way goblins every few minutes, and soon 100% of the goblins are apprehended.

Richard's technical friends note that this solution for identifying intruders is ridiculous, since the computer is already identifying intruders and depicting them in the game. The point in the experiment, as Richard explains, is that the game proves that such a platform works for crowdsourcing boring jobs.

You may want to think about how Stephenson's analogy extends to network intrusion detection experiments. Beyond gamification and crowdsourcing, how could you test the idea? What would the important variables be?

False Positives and False Negatives

False positives and false negatives are both errors that occur in imperfect systems and analysis, and arise often in scientific analysis. A false positive occurs when you, your analysis, or your solution incorrectly identifies the *presence* of an event or phenomenon when it was actually absent. A false negative occurs when you, your analysis, or

---

2 Bernhard Amann, Robin Sommer, Aashish Sharma, and Seth Hall. "A lone wolf no more: supporting network intrusion detection with real-time intelligence." In *Proceedings of the 15th international conference on Research in Attacks, Intrusions, and Defenses* (RAID'12), Davide Balzarotti, Salvatore J. Stolfo, and Marco Cova (Eds.). Springer-Verlag Berlin, Heidelberg (2012), 314-333.

your solution incorrectly identifies the *absence* of an event or phenomenon when it was actually present.

Let's start with a noncybersecurity example. You go to the doctor and are told that you've tested positive for ycanthropy and that the test is 99% accurate. But 99% is the probability that if you have the disease then you test positive, not the probability that if you test positive then you have the disease. Because you hope that you don't have ycanthropy, you would like your test to be a *false positive*. Suppose that 0.1%—one out of every thousand people—actually have this rare disease. Table 5-1 illustrates real numbers instead of just percentages.

Table 5-1. True and false/positive and negative test results for lycanthropy

	Sick People	Healthy People	(totals)
Test result positive	99 (true positives)	999 (false positives)	1,098
Test result negative	1 (false negatives)	98,901 (true negatives)	98,902
(totals)	100	99,900	100,000

Consider intrusion detection. An IDS has a false positive if it raises an alarm for an intrusion when there was actually none present. Conversely, if the IDS has a false negative, an intrusion slipped through without detection. Both are undesirable. However, sometimes one is more undesirable than the other. In many cases, false positives and false negatives are balanced—that is, lowering one increases the other. In intrusion detection, a corporation may be unwilling to accept false negatives slipping through, and therefore tolerates a greater number of false positives. How many false positives or false negatives are acceptable depends on the situation.

 In an important paper, Stefan Axelsson applied the base-rate fallacy to intrusion detection systems and showed that a high percentage of false positives had a significant effect on a system's efficiency.[3] One could say that the "effectiveness" of an IDS depends not on its ability to detect intrusive behavior but on its ability to suppress false alarms.

Nobody but you can tell if something is a false positive or false negative in your network. Say you run Snort with the following rule, which detects denial-of-service attacks by alerting on traffic with the same source and destination IP address, and it is raising lots of alarms:

---

3 Stefan Axelsson. "The Base-Rate Fallacy and Its Implications for the Difficulty of Intrusion Detection," In *Proceedings of the 6th ACM Conference on Computer and Communication Security*, ACM Press, 1999, pp. 1–7.

```
alert ip any any -> any any (msg:"BAD-TRAFFIC same SRC/DST";
sameip; reference:cve,CVE-1999-0016;
reference:url,www.cert.org/advisories/CA-1997-28.html;classtype:bad-unknown;
sid:527; rev:4;)
```

Whenever you see lots of alarms from a rule, especially a newly added rule, you should take a careful look at the validity of the alarms. In this case, this rule is known to cause false positives due to normal Windows server traffic on UDP ports 137 and 138. If you didn't know this was a common false positive, you would look at the alarms and start by investigating the offending source IP. In this case, it is easy to mitigate the false positives by explicitly ignoring this rule for a Windows server (with IP 10.1.10.1):

```
alert ip !10.1.10.1 any -> any any (msg:"BAD-TRAFFIC same SRC/DST";
sameip; reference:cve,CVE-1999-0016;
reference:url,www.cert.org/advisories/CA-1997-28.html; classtype:bad-unknown;
sid:527; rev:4;)
```

To experiment with false negatives, you could generate packets that *should* violate the rule and send it past the IDS. If there is no alarm, you have a false negative and you should investigate why the traffic didn't match the IDS rule. Here is a command to test the rule used above using hping3, a versatile packet creation tool:

```
hping3 10.1.10.1 --udp --spoof 10.1.10.1
```

These errors are certainly not limited to intrusion detection. Anytime an imperfect system must answer binary (yes/no) questions about the presence or absence of a cybersecurity-related phenomenon, the false positive and negative rates should be calculated. Classical examples include antivirus (is this a virus?), log analysis (are these events correlated?), and network protocol identification (is this an SSL packet?).

Cybersecurity solutions in practice do not have 100% accuracy and therefore have some level of false positives and/or false negatives. The measurement of these types of errors is known as the *false positive rate* or *false negative rate*. These rates are probabilities over multiple comparisons. The false positive rate is as follows:

(False Positives) / *(False Positives + True Negatives)*

The false negative rate is here:

(False Negatives) / *(True Positives + False Negatives)*

In scientific literature, it is common to see a plot of the true positives and the false positives, known as a *receiver operating characteristic* (ROC) curve. The graph illustrates the accuracy of the system (called the detector) in single-detection tasks like intrusion detection. In Figure 5-1, you can see how the shape of the curve shows the accuracy of the system, with perfect accuracy in the top-left corner.

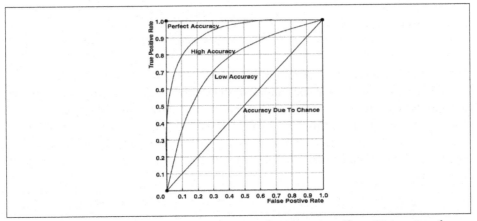

Figure 5-1. Ideal receiver operating characteristic (ROC) curves (from University of Newcastle (http://www.cs.newcastle.ac.uk/publications/trs/papers/871.pdf))

Sometimes it is possible to lower the false positive and false negative rates by sacrificing some other variable, such as performance. Giving the system additional time to calculate a more accurate result could be worth the trade-off, but experimentation is required to understand how much improvement in accuracy can be gained and whether users are willing to accept the added time cost. For evaluation purposes, it is useful to plot detection rate versus false alarms per unit time. These curves convey important information when analyzing and comparing IDSs. An IDS can be operated at any given point on the curve by tuning the system. Complex systems like IDS have many settings and configuration parameters that affect the system's overall accuracy. Stateful firewalls and intrusion detection systems require more computing power and complexity than stateless systems, but in most situations provide added security and lower false positives and negatives at an acceptable cost.

In the next section we will look at how to measure, test, and report on performance and two other attributes of cybersecurity solutions.

Performance, Scalability, and Stress Testing

Three attributes of cybersecurity products and solutions that are greatly important to users are performance, scalability, and resilience. Cybersecurity protections are often used in hostile environments where adversaries are actively working to break them down. Therefore, users of these defenses want to know how well the offering performs, how well it scales, and how it performs under stress. Buyers often use these attributes to compare products, and to judge products' value. There are many interpretations for defining and measuring these attributes and selecting the corresponding scientific measurements. Consider these examples:

- Our results suggest that keeping up with average data rates requires 120–200 cores.

- In the experimental evaluation, the two proposed techniques achieve detection rates in the range 94%–99.6%.

- Compared with the native Android system, OurDroid slows down the execution of the application by only 3% and increases the memory footprint by only 6.2%.

- Based on the data presented, the SuperSpeedy algorithm clearly outperforms the other AES finalists in throughput.

Each of these statements speaks differently about performance, and indirectly about scalability and resilience. In two cases, you see that the metric is given as a range rather than a single value. Reporting that an intrusion detection system, for example, has a 99% detection rate could be confusing or misleading because detection rates depend on many variables. This variability is also why scalability is important. Cloud computing is attractive to users because a fundamental tenant is the ability to handle unexpected (and expected) changes in demand.

Think about how your cybersecurity process or product changes the operating environment. These changes could improve the status quo, such as a time or memory speedup. Many solutions incur some kind of performance penalty to CPU usage, response time, throughput, etc. You should consider the penalty when using your solution in the average case *and* in the worst case. If you think that your solution incurs "low overhead," be prepared to defend that claim.

There are numerous performance benchmarks available today for a variety of use cases. Table 5-2 shows a few.

Table 5-2. Performance benchmarks

Performance benchmark	Description
Valgrind	Open source instrumentation framework for dynamic analysis, including a suite of performance benchmarks
Linpack	Measures computing power
Rodinia	Measures accelerated computing (e.g., GPUs)
netperf	Measures network traffic
CaffeineMark	Java benchmark
BigDataBench	Benchmark for scale-out workloads

In reality, most researchers don't use benchmark packages for measuring cybersecurity solutions. Reasons for this include cost and time, but low-cost and low-overhead alternatives are also available to allow you to gather data. In Linux, sysstat provides CPU utilization statistics that might suffice for your analysis. Many developers also create their own tools and techniques for measuring performance. Whatever you choose, be sure to report and adequately describe your methodology and results.

Here are two examples for benchmarking using built-in Linux tools. The first provides timing statistics about this program run. The second detects memory usage and errors.

```
[~] time ./program1

real    0m0.282s
user    0m0.138s
sys     0m0.083s

[~] valgrind --tool=memcheck ./program1
...
==8423== HEAP SUMMARY:
==8423==     in use at exit: 31,622 bytes in 98 blocks
==8423==   total heap usage: 133 allocs, 35 frees, 68,841 bytes allocated
==8423==
...
```

Case Study: Measuring Snort Detection Performance

In this section, we will walk through an experiment that measures Snort performance. Snort, the free and lightweight network intrusion detection package, was first introduced at the Large Installation System Administration (LISA) Conference in 1999. It has enjoyed widespread adoption around the world because of its powerful capabilities and open source distribution. Snort's primary feature is a rule-based signature engine and a rich language for creating signatures to detect activity of interest.

Building on Previous Work

Any practical deployment of Snort has many IDS signatures, possibly even hundreds or thousands. Snort's algorithms determine the order in which to check the input against the applicable rules. As you can expect, for any given input, the more rules that must be checked and the more computationally intensive the rules are, the slower the entire system performs.

A 2006 study by Soumya Sen confirmed this claim (Figure 5-2). The study author remarked, "The alarming fact about the growth in rule set is that larger rule sets implies more severe time constraints on packet handling and pattern matching by Snort, and failing to cope with this growing trend will mean severe performance deterioration and packet loss." IDS signature writers are very particular about optimizing rule performance and optimizing rule ordering. For example, defeat rules associated with broad categories of traffic are often processed first because they quickly decide whether there's a need to process additional rules. Even individual rules can be optimized; a rule which fires based on packet size and content is better optimized by checking the size first (a fast check) before searching the packet content for a match (a slow check). Today Snort has a performance monitor module and performance profiling tools for measuring real-time and theoretical maximum performance.

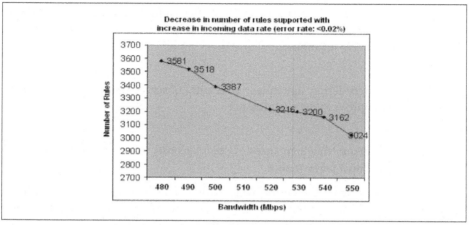

Figure 5-2. Dependence of bandwidth supported on rule set size (payload size: 1452 bytes) (from University of Minnesota (http://www.tc.umn.edu/~ssen/papers/ bell_labs_report_snort.pdf))

It might be useful to look at the experimental setup for another evaluation in which the researchers compared their new regular expression pattern matching algorithm to Snort and a commercial SIEM. Note the details about the test environment and the brief introduction to the metrics collected:[4]

> We conducted our experiments on an Intel Core2 Duo E7500 Linux-2.6.3 machine running at 2.93 GHz with 2 GB of RAM. We measure the time efficiency of different approaches in the average number of CPU cycles needed to process one byte of a trace file. We only measure pattern matching and submatch extraction time, and exclude pattern compilation time. Similarly, we measure memory efficiency in megabytes (MB) of RAM used during pattern matching and submatch extraction.

The authors provide specifications about the CPU, OS, and RAM because these details affect the outcome of the evaluation. It is important to record similar details for your experiments.

---

4 Liu Yang, Pratyusa K. Manadhata, William G. Horne, Prasad Rao, and Vinod Ganapathy. "Fast Submatch Extraction using OBDDs," In *Proceedings of the eighth ACM/IEEE symposium on Architectures for networking and communications systems* (ANCS '12). ACM, New York, NY, USA, 163–174.

A New Experiment

Consider a new hypothetical scientific experiment to dynamically reorder Snort rules based on historical usefulness. The intuition is that given a well-chosen set of individually optimized signatures, signatures that have alerted in the recent past are likely to appear again, and therefore should be checked early in the detection process. Here are null and alternative hypotheses:

H_0

Dynamically reordering signatures of recently observed alerts to the top of the list will not improve Snort performance.

H_1

Dynamically reordering signatures of recently observed alerts to the top of the list improves Snort performance.

You will want to compare the performance with and without reordering in order to decide if you should accept the hypothesis. As a control, you could use the results from Sen's study described above. However, this is unadvised because that study did not publish enough details about the rules used or experimental setup that would allow you to precisely compare your results (you can and should compare your results with that existing study). Instead, you should do a new control test to measure performance where the only variable change is dynamic rule reordering. Testing this hypothesis requires a prototype system that can do what we've described, namely reordering signatures in an intelligent way when Snort raises an alarm.

There are several ways to measure performance in this experiment. One would be to observe the effects on the allowable bandwidth throughput, as in Sen's study. Another choice would be measurement of changes to false positives and false negatives. A third choice would be measuring resource utilization such as memory and CPU load. There is no one right answer, and you may choose more than one set of measurements, but be sure to explain what, how, and why you measured the variables you did.

Figure 5-4 shows a graph that could show how reordering compares to the baseline. This graph shows that dynamic reordering allows you to have a greater number of rules than no reordering at the same network bandwidth. Say that you also measure the attacks detected and false alarms for Snort with and without dynamic reordering. The ROC curve in Figure 5-3 illustrates the comparison between the two systems and summarizes the relationship between false positive and detection probability. With these results, it's clear that for false alarm rates less than 55%, dynamic reordering increases detection. This is curious since both systems are using the same rules so you'd expect them to have identical ROC curves. We've discovered an interesting result that demands further investigation. At this point, it would be useful to set a new hypothesis about the cause and continue looking for the cause.

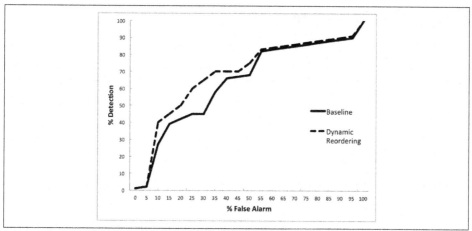

Figure 5-3. ROC curve of the percentage attacks detected versus the percentage of false alarms for Snort IDS with and without dynamic signature reordering

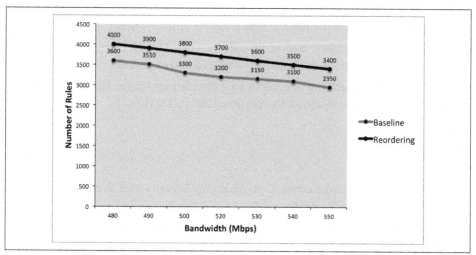

Figure 5-4. Bandwidth versus number of rules for Snort with and without rule reordering

If you've proven that dynamic reordering increases Snort performance, people will want to know and use your results. When you document and report the results of this experiment to your boss, team, or colleagues, you will include all the details necessary for another person to replicate the experiment. At a minimum, you would describe the experimental setup (hardware, network, rules used, network traffic source, and data collection instrumentation) and details about the algorithm for rule reordering. In the best case, you should publish or post online the exact Snort rule files used, source code for your modifications, and compilation and runtime commands.

How to Find More Information

Scientific research in this field is published and presented in general cybersecurity journals and conferences and at intrusion-specific venues including the International Symposium on Research in Attacks, Intrusions, and Defenses (RAID) and the Conference on Detection of Intrusions and Malware & Vulnerability Assessment (DIMVA).

Conclusion

This chapter explored cybersecurity science in intrusion detection and incident response. The key takeaways are:

- The need to respond and manage security incidents is a practical one, but also an area that can be improved through science.
- False positives and false negatives are errors in imperfect systems and analysis which arise in scientific analysis. Modifying intrusion detection systems and their signatures can adjust the rates of false positives and false negatives.
- Performance, scalability, and resilience are important to users of cybersecurity products and solutions. Each can be measured and evaluated.
- We applied cybersecurity science to an example experiment that measured performance related to dynamically reordered Snort IDS rules.

References

- Christopher Gerg and Kerry J. Cox. *Managing Security with Snort and IDS Tools.* (Boston, MA: O'Reilly, 2004)
- Henry H. Liu. *Software Performance and Scalability: A Quantitative Approach.* (Indianapolis, IN: Wiley, 2009).
- David J. Marchette. *Computer Intrusion Detection and Network Monitoring: A Statistical Viewpoint.* (Heidelberg: Springer, 2001)
- Zhenwei Yu and Jeffrey J. P. Tsai. *Intrusion Detection: A Machine Learning Approach.* (London: Imperial College Press, 2011)

## CHAPTER 6

Situational Awareness and Data Analytics

This chapter focuses on the application of science to cyber situational awareness, especially using big data. Awareness and understanding of what is happening on the network and in the IT environment is an important goal for infosec professionals because it allows us to confirm our security goals and quickly identify and respond to unanticipated and predetermined events. Yet, situational awareness is elusive. Our perception of cyber security is assembled from many data sources, not all of which are digital. If you want to know how IT is working in a hospital, you're as likely to know of an outage from users as from an automated email alert.

Situational awareness can come from information that is trivial or extraordinarily complex. To be sure that your web server is up, an automated process could simply scan it every minute and alert an admin when the scan fails. These kinds of binary checks—is it up or down?—are quite useful. Slightly more sophisticated checks come from counting. For example, the firewall seems to be dropping 90% of outbound traffic—I wonder why? Despite their simplicity, both of these types of checks, binary and counting, may still benefit from scientific experimentation.

You almost certainly need no help getting enough data about your network. There is little debate about the explosive growth of data in recent years and into the future. Humans are creating more and more digital artifacts like pictures, videos, and text messages. We are also creating technology that generates more and more digital information, from smartphones to telescopes. "Detecting misuse is also one area where the application of modern data-science practices may shine…," said the 2015 Verizon Data Breach Investigations Report. "All you need is data, features, and math." In cybersecurity, we often focus on analyzing machine data like server logs, transaction logs, and network logs. Researchers such as Roy Maxion (*http://www.cs.cmu.edu/ ~keystroke/*) at Carnegie Mellon University are using scientific experiments to look at new data sources, like the timing of keystrokes, that might help provide new sources of situational awareness for questions including "How sure are we that Bob is the one using the computer?"

An Example Scientific Experiment in Situational Awareness

For an example of scientific experimentation in situational awareness, see the paper "NStreamAware: Real-Time Visual Analytics for Data Streams to Enhance Situational Awareness" by Fischer and Keim.[1] In the following abstract, you can see a brief summary of a two-part software package that provides situational awareness using visualizations of summarized data streams. The implied hypothesis could be that "stream slices presented in a visual analytic application will enable a user to more effectively focus on relevant parts of the stream." These developers evaluated their solution with two case studies, one to demonstrate its usefulness in detecting network security events in an operational network and another with publicly available data from the 2014 VAST Challenge (*http://www.vacommunity.org/VAST+Challenge+2014*).

One important consideration to tool development is that users will probably use it in ways you didn't intend or foresee. The designers of NStreamAware showed two different use cases: network traffic and social media traffic. It is common and encouraged for researchers to think about use cases beyond the scope of the specific and intended use. By showing or describing the potential for extended uses of your scientific results or tools, you demonstrate the generality and usefulness of the solution. Some scientists call this "broader impact" to include benefits to other fields of science and technology.

Abstract from a situational awareness experiment
The analysis of data streams is important in many security-related domains to gain situational awareness. To provide monitoring and visual analysis of such data streams, we propose a system, called *NStreamAware*, that uses modern distributed processing technologies to analyze streams using *stream slices*, which are presented to analysts in a web-based visual analytics application, called *NVisAware*. Furthermore, we visually guide the user in the feature selection process to summarize the slices to focus on the most interesting parts of the stream based on introduced expert knowledge of the analyst. We show through case studies, how the system can be used to gain situational awareness and eventually enhance network security. Furthermore, we apply the system to a social media data stream to compete in an international challenge to evaluate the applicability of our approach to other domains.

---

1 Fabian Fischer and Daniel A. Keim. "NStreamAware: Real-Time Visual Analytics for Data Streams to Enhance Situational Awareness." In *Proceedings of the IEEE Conference on Visual Analytics Science and Technology (VAST)*, 2014.

The researchers describe their goal as an attempt to address the general problem of streaming data. "The challenge in this field is also to merge and aggregate heterogeneous high velocity data streams...," they write. "The ultimate goal allows the analysts to actually get an idea what is going on in a data stream to gain situational awareness." Others might have approached the problem by running analytics on a stored collection of data such as NetFlow records. In fact, it can seem confusing to figure out why a scientist took a particular approach or what led her to consider a certain hypothesis. As a researcher, I've learned that people are most excited about scientific results that apply to them, and that knowing what applies to them requires understanding their situation and challenges. Unexpected leaps in science can seemingly come from nowhere, but most scientific advances are incremental. As a practitioner, you have a unique advantage because you see and experience the work environment day-to-day. Your need to solve problems, combined with the curiosity to explore how or why things work, will produce a constant stream of testable hypotheses.

Want to get started with queries against large volumes of NetFlow? Here's an approach that uses NetFlow records stored in a Hadoop Distributed File System (*https://hadoop.apache.org*), the popular framework for distributed storage, and queries with Apache Hive (*https://hive.apache.org*), software for querying datasets in distributed storage:

1. Add NetFlow records to HDFS.

   ```
   [~] hadoop fs -mkdir /user/hadoop/data/netflow
   [~] hadoop fs -put /netflow/* /user/hadoop/data/netflow
   ```

2. Create and populate a table in Hadoop using the data you just added.

   ```
   [~] hive
   ```

   ```
   hive> create external table netflow (date1 string, date2 string, \
         sec string, srcip string, dstip string, srcport int, \
         dstport int, protocol string) row format delimited \
         fields terminated by ',' lines terminated by '\n' \
         stored as textfile location '/user/hadoop/data/netflow';
   ```

3. Query the table using Hive. Consider some experiments to compare the query times for using Hive compared to your current solution.

   ```
   hive> select * from netflow where srcip='10.0.0.33' limit 1;
   OK
   2015-06-10 22:14:07 2015-06-10 22:14:08 0.000 10.0.0.33 10.0.0.255 138
   138 UDP
   Time taken: 0.052 seconds, Fetched: 1 row(s)
   ```

4. You can imagine the richness that would come by adding other data sources, such as firewall, IDS, antivirus, database logs, and industry-specific logs like wire transfers and credit data. This is exactly what Zions Bancorporation did by mov-

ing three terabytes of data a week to Hadoop and MapReduce, decreasing query time from 20 minutes or more down to about one minute.[2]

Experimental Results to Assist Human Network Defenders

The goal of cybersecurity tools is to help humans carry out a particular function. We build tools to help us do our jobs faster, more effectively, and more safely. Automation is key to keeping up with the task volume we would otherwise have to attend to, and we now trust automated systems to act—and sometimes make decisions—on our behalf. Different organizations, countries, and cultures have different tolerances about the type and scope of automated responses. One organization may ignore unauthorized login attempts to the corporate VPN server, another may automatically blacklist the offending IP address or even scan it back.

One example where data analytics can aid humans with situational awareness is risk analysis. Nuanced questions such as "How much cyber-related risk are we accepting today?" are nontraditional for most companies but are enabled by advances in data analytics and machine learning. Interset (*http://bit.ly/1Nl3QZH*) is a Canadian company with the tagline "The science of threat detection." Interset sells a commercial solution that collects enterprise data and uses behavioral analytics for threat analysis. It writes in a whitepaper, "Big Data & Behavioral Analytics Applied to Security," (*http://bit.ly/1Nl3RNt*) about the mathematical model for behavioral analytics that it developed and implemented, which aggregates data about activities, users, files, and methods. End users can consume the results from these analytics with visual illustrations like the one in Figure 6-1.

---

2 Cloud Security Alliance (CSA) Big Data Working Group. *Big Data Analytics for Security Intelligence*, September 2013.

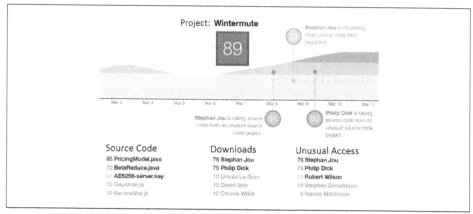

Figure 6-1. Interset visualization of risky behavior using behavioral analytics

Calculating cyber risk is complicated and not well understood today. You could conduct many scientific experiments to develop a risk equation that works for you. You might say "the more customer data we store in the database, the higher the risk that an attacker will try to steal the data." There are a great number of variables that affect this hypothesis including user training and countermeasures protecting the data. It would be extraordinarily complex to evaluate all the influential variables, but you can evaluate individual ones. Interset considers four factors (user, activity, file and method) in its model for behavioral risk. Using a ground-truth realistic dataset (your real network is unadvised), you could design your own risk equation and experimentally test to see how well it works.

Cognitive psychology tells us that humans aren't very good at judging probability or frequency of events. Given all the machines and users in your network, for example, which one is most likely to be attacked? Which one, if attacked, would cause the most downtime? The most financial impact? When Amazon.com went down in 2013, people speculated that they lost between $66,000–$120,000 per minute.

Drew Conway, author of *Machine Learning for Hackers*, describes data science as the intersection of hacking skills (e.g., file manipulation, algorithms), knowledge of math and statistics, and substantive expertise (Figure 6-2). While there is interesting science in each overlapping area, practical motivating questions and hypotheses come from substantive expertise, the grounding in the important real-world problems of a domain like cybersecurity. You don't necessarily need to possess all of these skills yourself. A team of three people, each with one skill area, can collaborate and produce strong results. Say you are a subject matter expert in DNS security and want to study the use of domain generation algorithms (DGAs), dynamically calculated Internet domain names used in malware like Conficker instead of hardcoded, static URLs for command and control. If you were monitoring DNS queries leaving your network, could you determine which ones came from humans and which came from malware with DGA? With the help of a statistician and a programmer you could calculate the distribution of alphanumeric characters in each DNS query and try to detect and categorize human-looking and algorithmically generated domains. This situational awareness could help identify malware in your network or explain other sources of nontraditional DNS traffic.

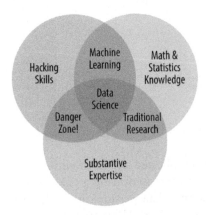

Figure 6-2. Drew Conway's data science Venn diagram (http://bit.ly/conway-data-venn)

No matter which combination of skills you possess for data science, machine learning is one of the broad fields you should be familiar with as you conduct tests and experiments for cybersecurity science. Machine learning offers features that nicely match the problems associated with situational awareness. The next section will summarize the important aspects of machine learning and how it might assist your scientific explorations.

Machine Learning and Data Mining for Network Monitoring

Machine learning is a scientific discipline, a multidisciplinary subfield of computer science, and a type of artificial intelligence. Speech recognition like Siri and Google now use an approach to machine learning (called neural networks) to enable machines to parse and understand human speech. In the past, computer scientists used static pattern-matching rules to parse data. Algorithms for machine learning, on the other hand, learn because their performance improves with experience without being explicitly reprogrammed. The more audio that a speech recognition algorithm processes, the more accurate it becomes. Machine learning is good at recognizing similar or variant things, not at identifying brand-new things. And remember, there is no one-size-fits-all machine learning solution, and the algorithms are only as good as the data they rely on.

Machine learning has many applications in cybersecurity solutions, from fraud detection to identifying high-risk employee behavior to intrusion detection and prevention. Here's a specific use case. Twitter cares a lot about detecting and preventing fake accounts, compromised accounts, and spam. Twitter might think that one way to detect fake accounts is by the number of tweets the account sends, and it could use machine learning to test that hypothesis. However, machine learning might reveal unexpected features of fake accounts, such as the mean time between tweets.

The field of machine learning is much too broad and complex for more than concise coverage here, but hopefully in this simple introduction you will come to understand its place in cybersecurity science and situations when machine learning might benefit you. There are many different machine learning techniques, so it is important to understand the ideas behind the various techniques in order to know how and when to use them. There is even a science to machine learning itself, and it is important to accurately assess the performance of a technique in order to know how well or how badly it is working.

In Chapter 2 we first looked at exploratory data analysis and suggested that visually looking at data could offer insights. *Clustering*, one approach to machine learning, is one way to look at data and to see if some of the data points are more similar to each other (grouped together in a cluster) than others. Clustering is one technique of *unsupervised learning*. That is, you or the machine learning algorithm are trying to find structure in unlabeled data. For example, finding clusters of malware families using only the executable and no other metadata could be accomplished with clustering. *Classification*, on the other hand, is a *supervised learning* approach. This task involves the use of labeled training data to teach an algorithm how to classify new examples. This technique is frequently used in image recognition where you tell the algorithm "these are 100 pictures of human faces" and ask "do you think this other picture is a face?"

As an experiment, say you want to cluster 15,000 possibly infected IP addresses. Organizing malware into homogeneous clusters may be helpful to generate a faster response to new threats and a better understanding of malware activities, since homogeneity in a cluster can be linked to similarity. As a data point, each infected IP address has associated features, some of which will be useful and others not. Using a chi-square test for feature selection, a statistical test used to test the independence of two events, you narrow down to 15 relevant features. Then, using the *k*-means clustering algorithm you find five distinct clusters of similarity among the infected hosts. *k*-means is an extremely popular clustering algorithm that attempts to partition data points into some number of clusters (*k* of them) in which each data point belongs to the cluster with the nearest mean. The algorithm does this by picking points that have a good chance of being in different clusters, and then assigning the other data points to the closest cluster based on a calculation of the distance of that point to the center of the cluster.

Looking for sample data to experiment with machine learning? There are 320 datasets (including 91 in computer science/engineering) in the UC Irvine Machine Learning Repository (*https://archive.ics.uci.edu/ml/datasets.html*).

One of the fastest ways to get started with machine learning is using R and the RStudio IDE. Despite a steep learning curve, R provides a free, high-quality environment for data analysis. In addition to a large number of functions, included features such as graphing are quite useful. Similar popular machine learning software includes Weka, Apache Mahout, and Apache Spark.

With the spread of cloud computing, machine learning is now available as a service! Azure Machine Learning and Amazon Machine Learning require little cost and expertise and offer enormous scalability. Both of these offerings guide users through questions that drive the process. Amazon Machine Learning currently supports three types of machine learning categories: binary classification, multiclass classification, and regression. Azure Machine Learning offers algorithms in regression, classification, clustering, and anomaly detection. Its algorithm cheat sheet can guide you through selecting the appropriate algorithm based on the kind of question or data you have (Figure 6-3).

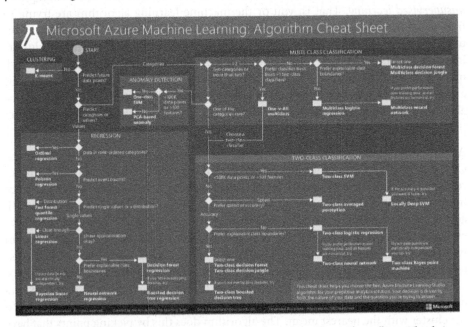

Figure 6-3. Microsoft Azure Machine Learning Algorithm Cheat Sheet (http://bit.ly/1Nl3Jxr)

No one algorithm in machine learning is appropriate for all problems; the chosen algorithm has to fit the problem. In mathematical folklore are two so-called no free lunch theorems that state if an algorithm performs well on one problem (or class of problems), then it pays for that with degraded performance on the set of all other problems. The takeaway is that because no algorithm is better than all others, you need to use as much problem-specific knowledge as possible in selecting an algorithm.

$16,000 Malware Classification Challenge

From February 2015 to April 2015, Microsoft sponsored a challenge on Kaggle (*https://www.kaggle.com/c/malware-classification*), the website for predictive modeling and analytics competitions. For the challenge, participants were given almost half a terabyte of data and asked to predict the probabilities that each file belonged to one of nine malware families. A total of 377 teams participated, and the top three teams received cash prizes totaling $16,000.

The winning team found three types of features that, when combined, enabled it to win the competition: opcode n-grams, line counts in binary segments, and pixel intensity from images created from ASM versions of the input files. In total the team found 15,000 features, narrowed to 2,193 after random forest selection. It wrote all of its code in Python.

Case Study: How Quickly Can You Find the Needle in the Haystack?

Malicious activity in a computer network is almost always like a needle in a haystack. The bad activity represents a very small percentage of total activity, and may even actively try to camouflage itself. A great deal of research, product development, and training have gone into this problem over time, and we have still not solved it. A 2010 DARPA test of six commercial security information and event management (SIEM) systems reported that no system could identify "low and slow" attacks, those with low activity volumes that occur slowly over time.[3] In fact, attack detection that we could call *finding needles* was the "single weakest area evaluated." How could you use scientific experimentation applied to network data to find more needles?

Say you use Nagios (*https://www.nagios.org*), the popular open source network monitoring program, for situational awareness of your moderately sized network and it generates 5,000 events per week. Many of those correspond to normal infrastructure

---

3 SPAWAR for DARPA/I2O. *Independent Validation and Verification (IV&V) of Security Information and Event Management (SIEM) Systems: Final Report*, 2010.

events, and your administrators are overwhelmed and ignore or filter the notifications. What if you could add value to your security operations by adding analytics to learn to detect anomalies and uncover "low and slow" malicious activity? This sounds like an opportunity for a summer intern that you can mentor through the scientific discovery process!

A New Experiment

Consider a hypothetical experiment to explore adding data analytics to Nagios that would automatically learn and detect outliers. Your intuition is that the network performs in a generally regular manner, and that anomalies to the norm can be detected even if they occur "low and slow." Here is a hypothesis:

> Adding machine learning to Nagios will find more true positive anomalies than Nagios and human analysts alone.

In this experiment, we must show that machine learning, the dependent variable, increases the number of anomalies found. This kind of experiment is difficult to conduct on live networks because you do not definitively know how many anomalies there are. A better choice for this experiment is to simulate a live environment but use data for which we know the precise number of anomalies. In the control group are Nagios and human analysts, and we must measure how many anomalies they can discover.

Time is an interesting factor in this experiment. You need to bound the time given to the human analysts. However, the humans bring years of training and experience, and the machine learning algorithms require time and experience to learn what normal and anomalous activity looks like in the data. It seems only fair that the algorithm should be allowed some training time without incurring a penalty in the experiment.

There are many ways to add machine learning to Nagios. As a developer and designer, you'll have to decide whether to use an algorithm that learns incrementally as new data streams by, or to periodically retrain the algorithm with a batch algorithm. Both are potentially interesting, and might yield experiments to compare the approaches. Your choice depends in part on how quickly you need new data to become part of your model, and how soon old data should become irrelevant to the model. These would also make for interesting experimental tests. Assume that you decide to implement an incremental algorithm and call the new solution NagiosML.

The execution of the experiment might go as follows. Five experienced network analysts are given one hour with Nagios and the test data and asked to identify the anomalies. Say there are 10 anomalies and the analysts find 7 on average. Then we train NagiosML with training data that contains 10 different anomalies. Once trained, five different network analysts are given an hour with NagiosML and the test data with which they also attempt to identify the anomalies. Say this time the analysts find eight on average but also two false positives. We have accepted the hypothesis as stated.

Nevertheless, the practical implications of the result are also important. The hypothesis did not ask to consider false positives, but in reality they cause added work to investigate. Users will have to decide whether finding an extra anomaly outweighs two false positives. You may also consider tweaking the algorithm and re-running the experiment to try to improve the detection rate and lower the error rate.

How to Find More Information

Advances and scientific results are shared at cybersecurity and visualization workshops and conferences. The first International Conference on Cyber Situational Awareness, Data Analytics, and Assessment (CyberSA) took place in 2015. Importantly, situational awareness is not limited to cybersecurity, and we have much to learn from other fields, from air traffic control to power plants to manufacturing systems.

Conclusion

This chapter covered cybersecurity science for situational awareness and data analysis. The key takeaways are:

- Cybersecurity science can guide experiments that evaluate how well a solution is helping human network defenders achieve a particular goal.

- It takes a combination of skills and expertise to conduct experiments in data science, and a collaborative team can produce strong results.

- Machine learning is good at recognizing similar or variant things and has many applications in cybersecurity solutions, from fraud detection to identifying high-risk employee behavior to intrusion detection and prevention.

- We set up an experiment to evaluate the hypothesis that adding machine learning to Nagios network monitoring software would find more true positive anomalies than Nagios and human analysts alone.

References

- Richard Bejtlich. *The Practice of Network Security Monitoring* (San Francisco, CA: No Starch Press, 2013)

- Michael Collins. *Network Security Through Data Analysis: Building Situational Awareness* (Boston, MA: O'Reilly, 2014)

- Peter Harrington. *Machine Learning in Action* (Shelter Island, NY: Manning Publications, 2012)
- Gareth James, Daniela Witten, Trevor Hastie, Robert Tibshirani. *An Introduction to Statistical Learning: with Applications in R* (Heidelberg: Springer, 2013)
- Chris Sanders and Jason Smith. *Applied Network Security Monitoring: Collection, Detection, and Analysis* (Waltham, MA: Syngress, 2013)
- Ian H. Witten, Eibe Frank, Mark A. Hall. *Data Mining: Practical Machine Learning Tools and Techniques* (Waltham, MA: Morgan Kaufmann, 2011)

## CHAPTER 7

Cryptography

Cryptography may be a science unto itself, but it also plays a major role in the science of cybersecurity. Bruce Schneier described it this way: "Traditional cryptography is a science—applied mathematics—and applied cryptography is engineering." Gauss famously called mathematics "the queen of the sciences." Like other sciences, there are pure mathematics (with no specific application in mind) and applied mathematics (the application of its knowledge to applications and other fields).

Whether cryptography *is* a science, there is value in looking at how to *use* the scientific method to evaluate the design and application of cryptography. In this chapter, we will look at provably secure cryptography. However, those proofs have limitations because the proofs deal with very specific attacks. And despite provable security, people break or find flaws in cryptographic systems all the time. They're broken because of flaws in implementation, a true and often cited reason. Cryptographic systems also suffer from defects in other noncryptographic systems, such as cryptographic keys left unsecured in memory, lazy operating system practices, and side-channel attacks (information leaks from the physical hardware running the cryptography).

Though there are open problems in the mathematical aspects of cryptography, you are more likely interested in ways to use cybersecurity science to evaluate and improve products and services. So, in this chapter we will ignore the fundamental mathematical construction of cryptographic algorithms and focus on their implementation and performance.

An Example Scientific Experiment in Cryptography

For an example of cybersecurity science in cryptography, look at the paper "SDDR: light-weight, secure mobile encounters" (*http://bit.ly/1Sm2YZD*) by Lentz et al. (2014). In the following abstract, you can see that an implied hypothesis is that

SDDR, the authors' new protocol for discovery of nearby devices, is provably correct and at least as energy-efficient as other proven cryptographic protocols. These developers took a two-pronged approach in their evaluation with both formal proof of security and experimental results of its energy efficiency using a research prototype. This combined approach appeals to a wider audience than, say, a formal proof alone. Note that the abstract highlights "four orders of magnitude more efficient" in energy-efficiency and "only ~10% of the battery," though readers must draw their own conclusions about the impressiveness of those results.

Abstract from an experiment of cybersecurity science in cryptography

Emerging mobile social apps use short-range radios to discover nearby devices and users. The device discovery protocol used by these apps must be highly energy-efficient since it runs frequently in the background. Also, a good protocol must enable secure communication (both during and after a period of device co-location), preserve user privacy (users must not be tracked by unauthorized third parties), while providing selective linkability (users can recognize friends when strangers cannot) and efficient silent revocation (users can permanently or temporarily cloak themselves from certain friends, unilaterally and without re-keying their entire friend set).

We introduce SDDR (Secure Device Discovery and Recognition), a protocol that provides secure encounters and satisfies all of the privacy requirements while remaining highly energy-efficient. We formally prove the correctness of SDDR, present a prototype implementation over Bluetooth, and show how existing frameworks, such as Haggle, can directly use SDDR. Our results show that the SDDR implementation, run continuously over a day, uses only ~10% of the battery capacity of a typical smartphone. This level of energy consumption is four orders of magnitude more efficient than prior cryptographic protocols with proven security, and one order of magnitude more efficient than prior (unproven) protocols designed specifically for energy-constrained devices.

As a practitioner, how would you apply these research results or ideas if you saw this paper online or heard about it from a colleague? If you develop smartphone applications, you might be interested in incorporating this protocol into your own product. Thankfully, all of the research prototype code for SDDR is available on GitHub (*https://github.com/mattlentz/ebn-sddr*). Or, you may have a solution of your own already and wish to compare how your algorithm compares to SDDR. Or maybe you're curious or skeptical and want to replicate or extend the experimental results from this paper.

Experimental Evaluation of Cryptographic Designs and Implementation

One of the most common experimental evaluations in cryptography is of the performance of cryptographic algorithms. Cryptographers and practitioners compare algorithms in order to understand the algorithms' strengths, weaknesses, and features. Those results inform future cryptographic design and inform the choice of algorithm to use in a new cybersecurity solution. Figure 7-1 illustrates a comparison of throughput for six cryptographic algorithms. Other performance metrics in cryptography commonly include encryption time and power consumption. These results come from running the algorithm and measuring the relevant metric, perhaps with different input file sizes. It is critically important to report the type of hardware used for the experiment in these studies since hardware specifications, especially processors and memory, strongly influence cryptographic performance.

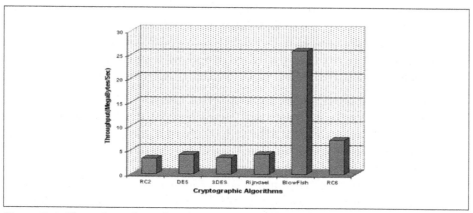

Figure 7-1. Throughput (megabytes/second) of six symmetric encryption algorithms from "Evaluating The Performance of Symmetric Encryption Algorithms" (2010)

There is value in experimental evaluation for cybersecurity implementations beyond a comparison of the algorithms themselves. Experimental evaluation of implementations and cryptography in practice are also possible. One could design an experiment to measure the lifetime of cryptographic keys in memory for different operating systems, or the usability of encryption features in email (see the case study in Chapter 11).

There are many other ways to evaluate cryptographic designs and implementations. Cryptanalysis attacks are used to evaluate the mathematical construction and practical implementation of cryptographic algorithms. Here are some common cryptographic attacks that can be used in experimentation:

Known-plaintext attack
   The attacker obtains the ciphertext of a given plaintext.

Chosen-ciphertext attack
   The attacker obtains the plaintexts of arbitrary ciphertexts of his own choosing.

Chosen-plaintext attack
   The attacker obtains the ciphertexts of arbitrary plaintexts of her own choosing.

Brute-force attack

    The attacker calculates every possible combination of input (e.g., passwords or keys) and tests to see if each is correct.

Man-in-the-middle attack

    The attacker secretly relays and possibly alters the communication between two parties who believe they are communicating directly with each other.

Cryptography is an answer to the problem of data protection. If you were given a new cybersecurity solution, say software for full disk encryption, how would you evaluate its effectiveness at doing what it claims and how would you validate whether you were any more secure from using it? These questions start to blur the line between cryptography and software assurance, not to mention risk management.

If you implement or test cryptography, keep several things in mind. First, in cryptography, Kerckhoffs's principle states that a cryptosystem should be secure even if everything about the system (except the key) is public knowledge. One implication of this principle is that cryptographic algorithms should be subject to peer review, not kept secret. Second, because cryptography implementers are often not cryptographers themselves, errors and shortcuts in implementation can weaken the cryptography.[1] Third, you should also pay attention to all the details of the protocol specification and check the assumptions attached to the cryptographic and protocol designs. Security assumptions are discussed in the next section. Finally, be aware that we are rarely sure if cryptography is completely secure. Acceptance of cryptography generally comes from long periods of failed attacks, and experimentation can uncover such cryptographic weaknesses.

Provably Secure Cryptography and Security Assumptions

In 1949, mathematician and father of information theory Claude Shannon wrote *A Mathematical Theory of Cryptography* and proved the perfect secrecy of the one-time pad. This notion of perfect secrecy means that the ciphertext leaks no information about the plaintext. The phrase *perfect secrecy* requires some explanation. *Information theory* is a collection of mathematical theories about the methods for coding, transmitting, storing, retrieving, and decoding information. Perfect secrecy is an information theoretic notion of security, which means that you can use mathematical theories to prove it.

---

1 As an example, an old version of GNU Privacy Guard (GPG) contained a flaw in the ElGamal crypto algorithm. The developer had this comment in the source code: "I don't see a reason to have a x of about the same size as the p. It should be sufficient to have one about the size of q or the later used k plus a large safety margin. Decryption will be much faster with such an x."

Information theory can even be used to describe the English language. Rules of grammar, for example, decrease the entropy (uncertainity) of English. For more, see Shannon's paper "Prediction and Entropy of Printed English." (*http://bit.ly/1Nl4aI5*)

As a practitioner, it is important to understand that provable security in information theory and cryptography is not an absolute statement of security. Security proofs are conditional and are not absolute guarantees of security. Security is guaranteed only as long as the underlying assumptions hold. Provable security is incredibly important because it brings a quantitative nature to security. This enables protocol designers to know precisely how much security they gets with the protocol.

Take SSH as an example. In 2002, three researchers conducted the first formal security analysis of the SSH Binary Packet Protocol (BPP) using the provable security approach.[2] Yet, other researchers later showed an attack on SSH BPP because the proven security model made some assumptions about the real-world system executing the decryption.[3] A very good research question comes from this example: how do we know that "fixing" SSH actually improves security? TLS/SSL, too, has been studied, and by 2013 there were papers showing that most unaltered full TLS ciphersuites offer a secure channel. The important words are *most*, *unaltered*, and *full*. No security analysis has yet shown that TLS is secure in all situations.

A security model is the combination of a trust and threat models that address the set of perceived risks. Every cybersecurity design needs a security model. You cannot talk about the security of a system in a vacuum without also talking about the threats, risks, and assumptions of trust. The work lies in determining what assumptions to include in a security model and how close the theoretical model is to the practical implementation to capture the significant attack vectors. To get you started thinking of assumptions on your own, here are a few potential assumptions about threats or attackers' technical abilities that could be made for a particular situation or environment:

- The adversary can read and modify all communications.

- The adversary has the ability to generate messages in a communication channel.

- The adversary has no ability to tamper with communication between the honest parties.

---

2 Mihir Bellare, Tadayoshi Kohno, and Chanathip Namprempre. 2002. "Authenticated encryption in SSH: provably fixing the SSH binary packet protocol." In *Proceedings of the 9th ACM conference on Computer and communications security* (CCS '02), Vijay Atluri (Ed.). ACM, New York, NY, USA, 1–11.

3 Martin R. Albrecht, Kenneth G. Paterson, and Gaven J. Watson. 2009. "Plaintext Recovery Attacks against SSH." In *Proceedings of the 2009 30th IEEE Symposium on Security and Privacy* (SP '09). IEEE Computer Society, Washington, DC, USA, 16–26.

- The adversary has the ability to spoof its identity.
- The adversary has the ability to leak from each key a few bits at a time.
- The adversary does not have access to the master key.
- The adversary has the ability to predict operations costs.
- The adversary has unlimited computing power.
- The adversary can mount login attempts from thousands of unique IP addresses.
- The adversary cannot physically track the mobile users.

Whenever you make a security claim, also describe any and all assumptions you make about the threat. It is disingenuous to assume an all-powerful adversary or to underestimate the capabilities of possible adversaries. In the next section we will talk about the Internet of Things (IoT), where we might assume that you are designing the security for smart clothing like a shirt with movement sensors woven into the fabric. Here is one example adversarial model for that situation:

> We assume that the adversary is interested in detecting a target's movement at all times, thereby violating a user's expected privacy. We assume that the adversary does not have physical access to his target's shirt. We assume that the adversary can purchase any number of identical shirts to study. We assume that any other shirt may be corrupted and turned into a malicious item controlled by the adversary. We assume that the adversary has the ability to infer all of the IoT items that belong together or to the same user.

This collection of assumptions bounds what we explicitly believe the adversary can and cannot do. The model usually contains only those motivations, capabilities, or limitations of the adversary pertinent to the security offered by the proposed solution. You might go on to suggest that the shirt needs SSL security because you can construct an attack that would otherwise succeed given the stated adversarial model.

Not only do attackers target cryptographic implementations, they also target the written and unwritten assumptions. Note that security models are not limited to cryptography. It is quite common for cybersecurity papers to include an entire section on the threat model used in the paper. The threat model narrows the scope of the scenario and may also limit the applicability of the attack or defense being presented. These can be very specific statements, such as "we assume that the adversary does not have any privileged access on any of the key network entities such as servers and switches, so she is unable to place herself in the middle of the stream and conduct man-in-the-middle attacks."

A well-defined security model benefits both the investigator conducting the assessment and the consumer of the final assessment. The model bounds the experiment and allows you to focus on a confined problem. It also establishes relevancy for the end user or consumer of your product.

Cryptographic Security and the Internet of Things

The proliferation of Internet-enabled devices has taken off more quickly than security measures for them. RSA Conference (*http://www.rsaconference.com*) is an annual information security event with a strong emphasis on cryptography. This is one of the largest events in the industry, with around 33,000 attendees and more than 490 sessions in 2015. Presentations follow industry trends, and there has been a clear rise recently in talks on the Internet of Things (IoT). Kaspersky Labs summarized the trend in 2015 as the "Internet of Crappy Things" (*https://blog.kaspersky.com/internet-of-crappy-things-2/*) highlighting a string of new attacks on home automation and other consumer devices.

Small resource-constrained devices such as insulin pumps require algorithms that respect their computing power, memory requirements, and physical size. In a world of desktops, laptops, and even smartphones, we could implement RSA, AES, and other mainstream algorithms with an acceptable burden on the device. But what about a smartcard, smart meter, medical implant, or soil sensor? What you can fit on the device and what the device needs are very different. IoT devices need efficient, lightweight cryptographic implementations that are also trustworthy. There are at least 24 lightweight block ciphers today designed with these constraints in mind. The National Security Agency even proposed two families of lightweight block ciphers called Simon (optimized for hardware) and Speck (optimized for software).[4] You can find a list of lightweight ciphers and their technical features (e.g., block size) on the CryptoLUX Wiki (*https://www.cryptolux.org/index.php/Lightweight_Block_Ciphers*).

Some have proposed offloading cryptographic functions in resource-constrained devices. A dedicated microcontroller might increase performance and reduce the load on the main CPU. It might also be possible to outsource crypto to a service on another device, as long as certain assurances were made.

Cybersecurity Jobs Requiring Scientific Curiosity

The following job description for Security Architect appeared recently for Nest, manufacturer of Internet-enabled devices such as cameras and thermostats. This role would benefit from an individual with the scientific skills we have discussed. While the position isn't a traditional research role and doesn't use the word "research" or "science," scientific thinking and cybersecurity experimentation would enhance the stated work objectives.

---

[4] Ray Beaulieu, Douglas Shors, Jason Smith, Stefan Treatman-Clark, Bryan Weeks, and Louis Wingers. The SIMON and SPECK Families of Lightweight Block Ciphers (*http://eprint.iacr.org/2013/404.pdf*). Cryptology ePrint Archive, Report 2013/404, 2013.

Experimentation in cybersecurity science can be used to measure and evaluate design choices for a specific device or class of devices. Say you are investing in a home automation system and want to add tiny soil moisture sensors that alert you when to water your plants. How would you decide how much wireless security was necessary, and whether the sensors could handle it? Deciding on the amount of security takes us back to the discussion in the previous section about threat models and assumptions. You must think about the different security threats and their associated likelihood. For example, do you care about physical attacks like node capture, impersonation attacks, denial-of-service attacks, replay attacks, or spoofing attacks? If you do care, what is the likelihood of them, and what is the cost of damage if any occur? We've just outlined a risk analysis that isn't very technical but is nonetheless critical. On the technical side, how could you also determine how well the sensors could even perform the desired level of cryptography? These technical considerations are reflected in the case study in the next section.

Another example of IoT devices to consider is smart utility sensors such as water and electric meters. These devices are being offered (sometimes mandated) for both consumers and businesses. Smart meters effectively increase the attack surface because the devices are networked together or back to the provider. Today, consumers have little choice but to treat such devices as black boxes without knowledge of how they work. Experimentation and evaluation with the scientific method will allow users to determine the cybersecurity assurances and risks associated with smart meters.

Case Study: Evaluating Composable Security

Background

The security of individual electronic devices has evolved significantly over time, followed by the growth of security for systems of devices such as corporate networks. A logical next question is "what is the impact to systemwide security given the assembly of individual components or subsystems?" This area of study is called *composable security*. Here's one example. If I trust the security of my Fitbit fitness tracker on its own, and trust the security of my iPhone on its own, and trust the security of the WiFi in my home, are any of those individual devices or the group of them any less (or more) secure because of their interconnectedness? The unexpected properties that arise or emerge from the interaction between the components are sometimes called *emergent properties*. Emergent properties are value-neutral; they are not inherently positive or negative, but because of their unexpected nature we often think of them as harmful.

For more coverage on composable security, including a discussion on challenges of emergent phenomena to risk assessment, see *Emergent Properties & Security: The Complexity of Security as a Science* (*http://dl.acm.org/citation.cfm?id=2683468*) by Nathaniel Husted and Steven Myers.

Both cybersecurity offense and defense can have emergent properties. Emergent attacks are created because a group of individual agents form a system that achieves an attack made possible by the collaboration. Distributed denial-of-service (DDoS) is an example of this; a single bot does not have much effect, but the combined forces of many bots in a botnet produce devastating results. You could run scientific experiments to measure the spectrum of these emergent effects as the size of the attacking swarm grows. Emergent defenses also arise due to the composition of some property of a group. Anonymity is an emergent property that is not apparent in isolation. The anonymity of Tor is a property that manifests as the system grows; a single Tor node does not achieve the same level of defense as a large collection of nodes. This fact is easy to demonstrate scientifically by showing the ability to violate anonymity in a one-node Tor network and the difficulty in doing so in a ten-node Tor network.

There is a very special instantiation of composable security for cryptographic protocols, known as *universal composability*. Universally composable cryptographic protocols remain secure even if composed with other instances of the same or other protocols. In 2008, scholars presented a security analysis of the Transport Layer Security (TLS) protocol under universal composability.[5] On the contrary, there are multi-party cryptographic protocols that are provably secure in isolation but are not secure when executed concurrently in larger systems. Further, there are classes of functions that cannot be computed in the universally composable fashion.

A New Experiment

The evaluation of composable security and emergent properties remains an open problem, but let us consider a hypothetical experiment to test a particular use case. This problem deals with the establishment of secure communication paths in IoT networks.[6] Rather than relying on theoretical analysis, we focus on practical feasibility and an experimental setup for the verification of runtime behavior. Here is a hypothesis:

> Three ad hoc IoT devices can establish secure communication paths whose composed communication security is equivalent to the security of two.

The intuition here is that we want to show (a) that two ad hoc devices can establish secure communications and (b) that by adding a third, communications are no less secure.

The probability of establishing communication between any pair of nodes in an ad hoc network is an emergent property of random graphs and has been studied since the 1960s.

As a practical experiment, it is acceptable to select three specific IoT devices you care about for the test as opposed to trying to prove a theoretical result that holds for any three devices. This approach does carry a limitation that the result may not be generalizable, and it is worth noting that when sharing your results. You should also consider using three devices of the same type, since mixing device types introduces complexity and additional variables into the experiment. For this study, let's use three Pinoccio Scouts (*https://pinocc.io*). These tiny and inexpensive devices are ideal because they natively support mesh networking and are built with open source software and hardware. Scouts use the Lightweight Mesh protocol, and that protocol supports two encryption algorithms: hardware accelerated AES-128 and software XTEA. However, the entire network uses the same shared encryption key by default.

---

5 Sebastian Gajek, Mark Manulis, Olivier Pereira, Ahmad-Reza Sadeghi, and Jorg Schwenk. "Universally Composable Security Analysis of TLS—Secure Sessions with Handshake and Record Layer Protocols." In *Proceedings of the 2nd International Conference on Provable Security (ProvSec '08)*, Joonsang Baek, Feng Bao, Kefei Chen, and Xuejia Lai (Eds.). Springer-Verlag, Berlin, Heidelberg, 313-327, 2008.

6 This problem is based on one offered by Virgil D. Gligor in *Security of Emergent Properties in Ad-Hoc Networks* (*http://www.ece.umd.edu/~gligor/cambridge04.pdf*).

An important result that you could demonstrate deals with key management. Obviously, having the same encryption key for all nodes leads to a rejection of the hypothesis because compromising the communication key in a two-node network *decreases* the composed security of a three-node network. You would have to implement a key exchange protocol that doesn't rely on external public key infrastructure and respects the limited memory of the nodes and their inability to store keys for a large number of peers. Using your knowledge of cybersecurity, you also want to consider potential ways that secure communication might be compromised: physical layer vulnerabilities, link layer jamming, passive eavesdropping, spoofing attacks, replay attacks, routing attacks, flooding attacks, and authentication attacks. It is your discretion about which of these you think need to be addressed in the security demonstration. Furthermore, for each one, you must now think about the difference between two-node networks and three-node networks, and the security differences between those cases. Unlike the shared encryption key, perhaps you argue that jamming attacks are no more disruptive to the secure communication paths of two nodes than three.

How to Find More Information

Research in applied cryptography is presented at a large number of mathematics and cybersecurity conferences, including the USENIX Security Symposium, the International Conference on Applied Cryptography and Network Security (ACNS), and the International Cryptology Conference (CRYPTO). Likewise, research and experimental results appear in an assortment of journals and magazines, notably the *Journal of Cryptology* and *IEEE Transactions on Information Forensics and Security*. The Cryptology ePrint Archive (*http://eprint.iacr.org*) also provides an electronic archive of new results and recent research cryptography.

Conclusion

In this chapter, we looked at how to use the scientific method to evaluate the design and application of cryptography. The key takeaways are:

- One of the most common experimental evaluations in cryptography is the performance of cryptographic algorithms, including encryption time and power consumption.

- Provably secure cryptography and security proofs are conditional and are not absolute guarantees of security. Security is guaranteed only as long as the underlying assumptions hold.

- A security model is the combination of a trust and threat models that address the set of perceived risks. Every cybersecurity design needs a security model.

- Scientific evaluation of cryptographic algorithms is important in resource-constrained IoT devices.

- The evaluation of composable security and emergent properties remains an open problem. We looked at a hypothetical experiment to test secure communications in IoT networks.

References

- Ran Canetti. Universally Composable Security: A New Paradigm for Cryptographic Protocols (*https://eprint.iacr.org/2000/067.pdf*), *Cryptology ePrint Archive*, Report 2000/067, (July 16, 2013)
- Bruce Schneier and Niels Ferguson. *Cryptography Engineering: Design Principles and Practical Applications* (Indianapolis, IN: Wiley, 2010)
- Al Sweigart. *Hacking Secret Ciphers with Python* (Charleston, SC: CreateSpace Independent Publishing, 2013)

## CHAPTER 8

Digital Forensics

Digital forensics holds a unique distinction among the group of cybersecurity fields in this book because it *requires* science. Forensic science, by definition, is the use of scientific tests or techniques in connection with the detection of crime. There are many corporate investigators who use forensic-like tools and techniques for nonlegal uses such as internal investigations and data recovery, but the requirement for scientific rigor in those cases may be less demanding. In this chapter, we will talk about cybersecurity science in digital forensics, especially for tool developers, by exploring the requirements for scientific evidence in court, the scientific principle of repeatability, and a case study highlighting the differences between laboratory and real-world experiments.

The forensics community has a small but active international research community. There is a much larger population of digital forensic practitioners who use forensic tools and techniques to analyze digital systems but do not perform experimentation as their primary job. The research community supports the practitioners by investigating new and improved ways to collect, process, and analyze forensic data. In recent years the topics of interest to researchers have included memory analysis, mobile devices, nontraditional devices (e.g., gaming systems), and big data mining.

An Example Scientific Experiment in Digital Forensics

For an instructive example that illustrates scientific experimentation in digital forensic tool development, look at the abstract for "Language translation for file paths" (*http://www.dfrws.org/2013/proceedings/DFRWS2013-5.pdf*) by Rowe, Schwamm, and Garfinkel (2013). This paper presents a new tool and the experimental evaluation of its accuracy. In the abstract that follows, you can see that the first line of the abstract identifies the problem that these researchers were looking to address: forensic investigators need help understanding file paths in foreign languages. The implied hypothesis is that directory-language probabilities from words used in each directory name over a large corpus, combined with those from dictionary lookups and character-type distributions, can infer the most likely language. The authors give their contributions and results, including the sample size and accuracy. The test data (*http://digitalcor pora.org/corpora/disk-images/real-data-corpus*) is available to other researchers who might want to repeat or build upon these results, and the methodology is described in sufficient detail to enable other researchers to reproduce the experiment.

Abstract from a digital forensics experiment

Forensic examiners are frequently confronted with content in languages that they do not understand, and they could benefit from machine translation into their native language. But automated translation of file paths is a difficult problem because of the minimal context for translation and the frequent mixing of multiple languages within a path. This work developed a prototype implementation of a file-path translator that first identifies the language for each directory segment of a path, and then translates to English those that are not already English nor artificial words. Brown's LA-Strings utility for language identification was tried, but its performance was found inadequate on short strings and it was supplemented with clues from dictionary lookup, Unicode character distributions for languages, country of origin, and language-related keywords. To provide better data for language inference, words used in each directory over a large corpus were aggregated for analysis. The resulting directory-language probabilities were combined with those for each path segment from dictionary lookup and character-type distributions to infer the segment's most likely language. Tests were done on a corpus of 50.1 million file paths looking for 35 different languages. Tests showed 90.4% accuracy on identifying languages of directories and 93.7% accuracy on identifying languages of directory/file segments of filepaths, even after excluding 44.4% of the paths as obviously English or untranslatable. Two of seven proposed language clues were shown to impair directory-language identification. Experiments also compared three translation methods: the Systran translation tool, Google Translate, and word-for-word substitution using dictionaries. Google Translate usually performed the best, but all still made errors with European languages and a significant number of errors with Arabic and Chinese.

This example illustrates one kind of scientific experiment involving digital forensic tools. Such experiments could be done for other new tools, including those beyond digital forensics. In the next section, we will discuss the unique requirements for digital forensic tools because of their involvement in the legal process.

Scientific Validity and the Law

Digital evidence plays a part in nearly every legal case today. Even when the suspect is not attacking a computer system, he or she is likely to have used a cellphone, camera, email, website, or other digital medium that contains some bit of information relevant to investigation of a crime. It is important for forensic scientists to understand how the legal system deals with scientific evidence, and the unique requirements that the law imposes on tool development and scientific validity.

Scientific knowledge is presented in court by expert witnesses. Two Supreme Court decisions provide the framework for admitting scientific expert testimony in the United States today. The *Daubert* standard, from *Daubert v. Merrell Dow Pharmaceuticals* (1993) is used in federal cases and many states, though the *Frye* standard, from *Frye v. United States* (1923), is still used in the other states. *Daubert* says that scientific knowledge must be "derived by the scientific method." It continues in the same way that we previously discussed the scientific method, saying "scientific methodology today is based on generating hypotheses and testing them to see if they can be falsified."

According to *Daubert*, scientific evidence is valid and can be admitted in court when it adheres to testing, peer review, the existence of a known error rate or controlling standards, and the general acceptance of the relevant scientific community. These are important to remember as a digital forensic practitioner, developer, or researcher. Note that these standards deal with the method used to reach a conclusion, not the tool itself, though questions are often raised about the implementation or use of tools. The regulation of scientific evidence is unique to the United States, though it has been used in two Canadian Supreme Court cases and proposed in England and Wales. International law used between nations has few restrictions on the admissibility of evidence, and free evaluation of evidence in court prevails.

It is insightful to observe exactly how expert witness and tool validation plays out in the courtroom. Below is an excerpt of court testimony from *United States of America v. Rudy Frabizio* (2004), in which Mr. Frabizio was charged with possession of child pornography.[1] In this exchange, attorney Dana Gershengorn asks the witness, Dr. Hany Farid, questions seeking to establish general acceptance of the science of steganography:

> Q. Professor Farid, is the science underlining your work in steganography, that is, the patterns and the fact that they're distinguishable in images that have been tampered with by putting in covert messages as opposed to images that have not been so tampered, is that well accepted now in your field?
>
> A. Yes, it is.

---

1 Note: this is offered only as an example of the Daubert process. In 2006, a motion was filed to exclude this expert testimony. The memo stated, "The government initially offered Professor Hany Farid, a Dartmouth College professor of computer science and neuroscience. Professor Farid sought to distinguish real and computer-generated images through a computer, rather than using visual inspection. Farid's computer program purported to measure statistical consistencies within photographs and computer-generated images to determine whether or not an image was real. After one day of a hearing, the government withdrew Dr. Farid as an expert witness. Defense counsel noted that 30 percent of the time, Farid's program classified a photograph [i.e., a real image] as a computer-generated image, and she highlighted these errors. One stood out in particular: an image of a cartoon character, 'Zembad,' a surrealistic dragon, falsely labeled 'real.'"

Q. Is there any controversy on that that you're aware of, that is, that maybe these differences in statistics don't exist? Are you aware of any published material that contradicts that?

A. No.

Q. And is the technology that you've used in your steganography work, the program that you've used, is that the same technology, similar program that you used in examining images in the Frabizio case?

A. Yes, it is.

Later in the questioning, Dr. Farid describes the error rate for the software he used to analyze images in the case:

THE COURT: A fixed false positive rate means what now?

THE WITNESS: It means .5 percent of the time, a CG image, computer graphics will be misclassified as photographic.

Q. .5 percent of the time?

A. Yes, one in two hundred.

Q. Now, 30 percent of the time an image that is real, your program will say—

A. Is computer generated. Right. We need to be safe. We need to be careful. And, of course, you know, ideally the statistics would be perfect, they'd be 100 percent here and 100 percent here, but that's hard. We're moving towards that, but this is where we are right now.

Q. And in your field, having worked in this field for a long time and having reviewed other people's publications in peer review journals, is .5 percent accuracy acceptable in your field?

A. Yes.

This exchange illustrates the type of questioning that occurs in many court cases where digital evidence is presented. It may eventually happen with software you create if that software is used to produce evidence used in court! EnCase is one of the most widely used commercial software packages for digital forensics, and is routinely used to produce evidence used in court. Guidance Software, the makers of EnCase, has published a lengthy report that documents cases where EnCase was used and validated against the *Daubert/Frye* standards in court. You need not create such comprehensive documentation for every tool you create, but there are a few simple things you should do.

 Cybersecurity science in forensics that involves looking at potentially offensive, illegal, or personal information can raise complex legal and ethical issues. Consult an attorney or ethics professional to ensure that your experiments are safe, legal, and ethical. For more on human factors, see Chapters 11 and 12.

If you develop digital forensics software, and the evidence resulting from the use of your tools may be used in court, an expert witness may someday be asked to testify to the validity of your software. Here are a few things you can do to help ensure that your tools will be found valid in court, should the need arise:

- **Make your tools available.** Whether you develop free and open source software or commercial software, your software can only be tested and independently validated if it is available to a wide audience. Consider putting them on GitHub or SourceForge. As much as you are able, keep them up-to-date—abandoned and unmaintained tools may be discounted in court.

- **Seek peer review and publication.** It is important to the courts that your peers in the digital forensics community review, validate, and test your tools. This is an excellent opportunity for scientific experimentation. Publication is also one way to report on tests of error rates.

- **Test and document error rates.** No software is flawless. Apply the scientific method and objectively determine the error rates for your software. It is much better to be honest and truthful than to hide imperfections.

- **Use accepted procedures.** The courts want procedures to have "general acceptance" within the scientific community (this is commonly misunderstood to mean that the *tools* must have general acceptance). Open source is one way to show procedures you used, allowing the community to evaluate and accept them.

It may not be necessary to prepare every forensic tool and technique you create for the court. Following the scientific method and best practices in the field is always advised, and will help ensure that your tools are accepted and validated for court if the need arises.

Scientific Reproducibility and Repeatability

Reproducibility and repeatability are two important components for the evaluation of digital forensic tools and for scientific inquiry in general. *Reproducibility* is the ability for someone else to re-create your experiment using the same code and data that you used. *Repeatability* is about you running the test again, using the same code, the same data, and the same conditions. These two cornerstones of scientific investigation are too often overlooked in cybersecurity. A 2015 article in *Communications of the ACM* described their benefits this way: "Science advances faster when we can build on existing results, and when new ideas can easily be measured against the state of the art... Our goal is to get to the point where any published idea that has been evaluated, measured, or benchmarked is accompanied by the artifact that embodies it. Just as formal results are increasingly expected to come with mechanized proofs, empirical results should come with code."[2]

Consider a digital forensics technique that attempts to identify images of human beings in digital images. This is an important problem when investigating child pornography cases, and a computationally challenging problem to train a computer to identify images of humans. The developers of a new program, which contains a new algorithm for detecting human images, wish to show reproducibility and repeatability. They can show repeatability by running the same program several times, using the same input files, and achieving the same results. If the results vary, the experimenters must explain why. To achieve reproducibility, the developers should offer the exact program, the exact input files, and a detailed description of the test environment to others, allowing independent parties to show that they can (or cannot) achieve the same results as the original developers.

There are many challenges to reproducibility in cybersecurity and digital forensics. One obvious challenge is the incredible difficulty of ensuring identical conditions for different program runs. Computers are logical and predictable machines, yet replicating the exact state of a machine is nontrivial given their complexity. Sometimes the very act of doing an experiment changes the conditions, so documentation is critical. Virtual machine snapshots offer the ability to revert to an identical machine snapshot, but virtual machine guest performance may be affected by the host's performance (including other VMs running on the host).

A second significant challenge to reproducibility is that useful datasets are not widely available to researchers. As we saw in Chapter 2, there are a few repositories of available real, simulated, and synthetic test data. *DigitalCorpora.org* is a site specifically devoted to datasets for digital forensics research and contains various collections of disk images, packet captures, and files.

Case Study: Scientific Comparison of Forensic Tool Performance

In this section, we will walk through a hypothetical scientific experiment in digital forensics. In this experiment you are curious to know if parallel, distributed, cloud-based forensic processing using MapReduce can improve the speed of common forensic tasks. Given the volumes of data that forensic laboratories and analysts have to process, increased throughput would be valuable to the community. In your preliminary background reading, you find an implementation of the common open source forensic suite The Sleuth Kit for Hadoop (*http://www.sleuthkit.org/tsk_hadoop/*). Fur-

---

2 Shriram Krishnamurthi and Jan Vitek. *The real software crisis: repeatability as a core value (http://doi.acm.org/ 10.1145/2658987)*. Communications of the ACM 58, 3 (February 2015), 34–36.

ther, no performance data seems to exist, making this a new and interesting question to consider. You form your hypothesis as follows:

> The time required to construct a digital forensic timeline will be 75% faster using a Hadoop cluster than a traditional forensic workstation.

The independent variable in the hypothesis is the execution platform, which is a cloud and a desktop. You want to experimentally measure the execution time on both platforms, ensuring as much as possible that other variables are consistent. Therefore, you must use the same disk image in both cases for a fair test. You select a publicly available 500 MB USB drive image for this test. Because you wish to compare the benefit of parallel processing using TSK Hadoop, it would be wise to use comparable machine specifications so that one test is not unfairly advantaged by better hardware. Table 8-1 shows basic specifications for a single forensic workstation and 10 Amazon EC2 instances. The combination of the 10 EC2 instances is roughly equivalent to the workstation in CPU, memory, and storage. It is important to record and report the hardware specifications you used so that other researchers can replicate and validate your results.

Table 8-1. Example computer specs for performance comparison

Forensic workstation	Amazon EC2 instances (x10)
Dell Precision T5500	**T2 Small Type**
Ubuntu 14.04.1 LTS (64-bit)	Amazon Linux AMI (64-bit)
Dual Intel 6 Core Xeon X5650 @2.66GHz	1 Intel Xeon family vCPU @2.5GHz
24GB DDR3 Memory	2GB Memory
1TB 3.5″ 7200 RPM SATA	100GB EBS magnetic storage volume

Each run of the experiment will measure the execution time required for The Sleuth Kit to construct a timeline of the input drive image. You prepare both execution environments, run the process, and get a result. Because individual executions of a program are subject to many variables on the host computer (e.g., other background processes, etc.), you repeat the timeline creation five times to assure yourself that the results are consistent. This gives you the results in Table 8-2.

Table 8-2. Example times for timeline generation experiment

TSK on forensic workstation	TSK Hadoop on Amazon EC2
Run #1: 25 seconds	Run #1: 15 seconds
Run #2: 20 seconds	Run #2: 17 seconds
Run #3: 21 seconds	Run #3: 16 seconds
Run #4: 24 seconds	Run #4: 13 seconds
Run #5: 22 seconds	Run #5: 15 seconds

These results indicate that MapReduce runs approximately 33% faster on the 500 MB disk image. There were no extreme outliers, giving confidence to the data obtained. The data so far shows that you should reject your hypothesis, even though MapReduce is measurably faster. You now decide to test whether these results hold for different sizes of disk images. Using the Real Data Corpus (*http://digitalcorpora.org/ corpora/disk-images/rdc-faq*), you obtain one disk image each of size 1 GB, 10 GB, 500 GB, and 2 TB. You repeat the timeline creation five times for each disk image size, and graph the results as shown in Figure 8-1. As before, it appears that Hadoop is consistently faster than the single workstation, but not 75% faster as you hypothesized. At this point you could modify your hypothesis to reflect and apply your new knowledge. You could also extend the experiment with a new hypothesis and compare various Hadoop node sizes. Perhaps a five-node cluster performs as well as 10 in this case, or perhaps 20 nodes is substantially faster.

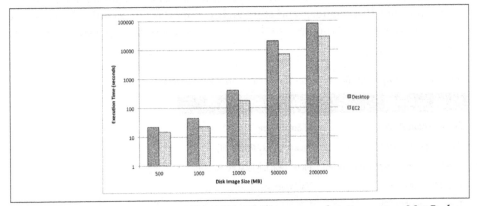

Figure 8-1. Example comparison of execution times on a workstation versus MapReduce for various disk image sizes

There are several ways to put your results to work. You should at least consider publishing your results online or in a paper. This preliminary data might be convincing enough to even start a company or build a new product that specializes in forensics as a service using MapReduce. At the very least you will have learned something!

How to Find More Information

Research is presented in general cybersecurity journals and conferences but also at forensic-specific venues including the Digital Forensics Research Workshop (DFRWS), IFIP Working Group 11.9 on Digital Forensics, and American Academy of Forensic Sciences. A popular publication for scientific advances in digital forensics is the journal *Digital Investigation*.

Conclusion

This chapter covered cybersecurity science as applied to digital forensics and forensic-like investigations and data recovery. The key takeaways are:

- Digital forensic scientists and practitioners must understand how the legal system deals with scientific evidence, and the unique requirements that the law imposes on tool development and scientific validity.

- According to *Daubert*, scientific evidence is valid and can be admitted to court when it adheres to testing, peer review, the existence of a known error rate or controlling standards, and the general acceptance of the relevant scientific community.

- Reproducibility is the ability for someone else to re-create your experiment using the same code and data that you used. Repeatability is the ability for you to run a test again, using the same code, the same data, and the same conditions.

- We explored an example experiment to study if cloud-based forensic processing could construct a forensic timeline faster than traditional methods.

References

- Eoghan Casey. *Digital Evidence and Computer Crime, Third Edition.* (Waltham, MA: Academic Press, 2011)

- *Digital Forensics Research Workshop (DFRWS) (http://www.dfrws.org)*

- *The Forensics Wiki (http://www.forensicswiki.org)*

- Cara Morris and Joseph R. Carvalko. *The Science and Technology Guidebook for Lawyers.* (Chicago, IL: American Bar Association, 2014)

## CHAPTER 9

Malware Analysis

The field of malware analysis is a prime candidate for scientific exploration. Experimentation is worthwhile because the malware problem affects all computer users and because advances in the field can be broadly useful. Malware also evolves over time, creating an enormous dataset with a long history that we can study. Security researchers have conducted scientific experiments that produced practical advances not only in tools and techniques for malware analysis but also in knowing how malware spreads and how to deter and mitigate the threat.

People who do malware analysis every day know the value of automation for repetitive tasks balanced with manual in-depth analysis. In one interview with [IN]SECURE, Michael Sikorski, researcher and author of *Practical Malware Analysis*, described his approach to analyzing a new piece of malware. "I start my analysis by running the malware through our internal sandbox and seeing what the sandbox outputs," followed by basic static analysis and then dynamic analysis which drive full disassembly analysis. Anytime you see the prospect for automation is the opportunity to scientifically study the process and later evaluate the improvements.

Recall from the discussion of test environments in Chapter 3 that cybersecurity science, particularly in malware analysis, can be dangerous. When conducting experimentation with malware, you must take extra precautions and safeguards to protect yourself and others from harm. We will talk more about safe options such as sandboxes and simulators in this chapter.

Malware analysis has improved in many ways with the help of scientific advances in many fields. Consider the disassembly of compiled binary code, a fundamental task in malware analysis. IDA Pro uses recursive descent disassembly to distinguish code from data by determining if a given machine instruction is referenced in another location. The recursive descent technique is not new, having been notably applied to compilers for decades and the subject of many academic research papers. Malware analysis tools, such as disassemblers, are enabled and improved through science.

An Example Scientific Experiment in Malware Analysis

For an example of scientific experimentation in malware analysis, look at the paper "A Clinical Study of Risk Factors Related to Malware Infections" (*http://dl.acm.org/cita tion.cfm?id=2516747*) by Lévesque et al. (2013). The abstract that follows describes an interesting malware-related experiment that looks not at the malware itself but at users confronted with malware infection. Humans are clearly part of the operating environment, including the detection of and response to malware threats. In this experiment, the researchers instrumented laptops for 50 test subjects and observed how the systems performed and how users interacted with them in practice. During the four-month study, 95 detections were observed by the AV product on 19 different user machines, and manual analysis revealed 20 possible infections on 12 different machines. The team used general regression, logistic regression, and statistical analysis to determine that user characteristics (such as age) were not significant risk factors but that certain types of user behavior were indeed significant.

Abstract from a malware analysis experiment

The success of malicious software (malware) depends upon both technical and human factors. The most security-conscious users are vulnerable to zero-day exploits; the best security mechanisms can be circumvented by poor user choices. While there has been significant research addressing the technical aspects of malware attack and defense, there has been much less research reporting on how human behavior interacts with both malware and current malware defenses.

In this paper we describe a proof-of-concept field study designed to examine the interactions between users, antivirus (anti-malware) software, and malware as they occur on deployed systems. The four-month study, conducted in a fashion similar to the clinical trials used to evaluate medical interventions, involved 50 subjects whose laptops were instrumented to monitor possible infections and gather data on user behavior. Although the population size was limited, this initial study produced some intriguing, non-intuitive insights into the efficacy of current defenses, particularly with regards to the technical sophistication of end users. We assert that this work shows the feasibility and utility of testing security software through long-term field studies with greater ecological validity than can be achieved through other means.

You can imagine that this kind of real-world testing would be useful for antivirus vendors and other cybersecurity solution providers. In the next section, we discuss the benefits of different experimental environments for malware analysis.

Scientific Data Collection for Simulators and Sandboxes

Experimental discovery with malware is a routine activity for malware analysts even when it isn't scientific. Dynamic analysis, where an analyst observes the malware executing, can sometimes reveal functionality of the software more quickly than static analysis, where the analyst dissects and analyzes the file without executing it. Because malware inherently interacts with its target, the malware imparts change to the target environment, even in unexpected ways. Malware analysts benefit from analysis environments, especially virtual machines, that allow them to quickly and easily revert or rebuild the execution environment to a known state. Scientific reproducibility is rarely the primary goal of this practice.

Different malware analysis environments have their own methods for collecting scientific measurements during experimentation. Commercial, open source, and home-grown malware-analysis environments provide capabilities that aid the malware analyst in monitoring the environment to answer the questions "what does this malware do and how does it do work?" One open source simulator is ns-3, which has built-in data collection features and allows you to use third-party tools. The ns-3 framework is built to collect data during experiments. Traces can come from a variety of sources which signal events that happen in a simulation.

A trace source could indicate when a packet is received by a network device and provide access to the packet contents. Tracing for pcap data is done using the `PointTo PointHelper` class. Here's how to set that up so that ns-3 outputs packet captures to *experiment1.pcap*:

```
#include "ns3/point-to-point-module.h"

PointToPointHelper pointToPoint;
pointToPoint.EnablePcapAll ("experiment1");
```

FlowMonitor is another ns-3 module that provides statistics on network flows. Here is an example of how to add flow monitoring to ns-3 nodes and print flow statistics.

```
// Install FlowMonitor on all nodes
FlowMonitorHelper flowmon;
Ptr<FlowMonitor> monitor = flowmon.InstallAll();

// Run the simulation for 10 seconds
Simulator::Stop (Seconds (10));
Simulator::Run ();

// Print per flow statistics
monitor->CheckForLostPackets ();
Ptr<Ipv4FlowClassifier> classifier = \
    DynamicCast<Ipv4FlowClassifier> (flowmon.GetClassifier ());
std::map<FlowId, FlowMonitor::FlowStats> stats = monitor->GetFlowStats ();
for (std::map<FlowId, FlowMonitor::FlowStats>::const_iterator i = \
    stats.begin (); i != stats.end (); ++i)
  {
    Ipv4FlowClassifier::FiveTuple t = classifier->FindFlow (i->first);
    std::cout << "Flow " << i->first << " (" << t.sourceAddress << " -> " \
            << t.destinationAddress << ")\n";
```

```
    std::cout << "  Tx Bytes:    " << i->second.txBytes << "\n";
    std::cout << "  Rx Bytes:    " << i->second.rxBytes << "\n";
    std::cout << "  Throughput: " <<
    i->second.rxBytes * 8.0 / 10.0 / 1024 / 1024 \
            << " Mbps\n";
}
```

It is easy to add software to collect measurements to sandboxes, especially in a virtual environment. You can install software on the virtual machine to collect network traffic, performance loads, and timing. There are now easily accessible tools for virtual machine introspection (VMI). VMI enables you to monitor the virtual machine from outside the machine using tools on the host. LibVMI (*http://libvmi.com*), for example, allows you to access the guests' memory and CPU state. The primary benefit is that the malware inside the guest virtual machine doesn't know this observation is happening. PyVMI is a Python adapter for LibVMI, which allows you to instrument data collection however you want. You can also use a PyVMI library with Volatility for runtime memory analysis.

```
[~]$ # Copy the PyVMI address space file to Volatility's plugins folder
[~]$ cp libvmi/tools/pyvmi/pyvmiaddressspace.py volatility/plugins/addrspaces/

[~]$ # Create a LibVMI profile for the virtual machine
[~]$ # Here is an example entry for a Windows 7 VM
[~]$ cat /etc/libvmi.conf
win7 {
    ostype = "Windows";
    win_tasks = 0xb8;
    win_pdbase = 0x18;
    win_pid = 0xb4;
}

[~]$ # Run Volatility and specifying the Xen VM ("win7") as the URN for the
[~]$ # address space
[~]$ python vol.py -l vmi://win7 pslist
```

Community Cybersecurity Science

Crowdsourced community science projects have enabled average citizens to participate in distributed science projects from the comfort of their home or backyard. SciStarter (*http://scistarter.com*) has more than 1,000 projects that citizen scientists can contribute to, from reporting bird sightings to counting bees. While few cybersecurity projects are currently hosted at SciStarter, the cybersecurity community has been working together through other means for many years.

Because malicious activity doesn't occur uniformly and simultaneously around the Internet, there is value in observing and collecting data from various vantage points around the globe. The Honeynet Project, for example, is an international nonprofit organization of volunteers who, since 1999, have collectively gathered and analyzed data about attackers and malware. The Honeynet Project has sponsored and supported many cybersecurity research projects including the Cuckoo malware sandbox.

Cybersecurity information sharing is growing in other ways, too. Industry providers like FireEye and Symantec share information with paying customers. The US Department of Homeland Security coordinates sharing between government and trusted industry partners. Other efforts like AlienVault Open Threat Exchange allow anyone to contribute anonymized threat information and receive community threat intelligence and data. While these programs are primarily designed for actionable cybersecurity, they may also be a resource for individual or global cybersecurity science.

Finally, there is an active culture promoting independent software bug hunting. Google, Facebook, Microsoft, and many other companies offer recognition, money, and other incentives to individuals who discover and report new bugs in their software. HackerOne provides a platform to connect bug hunters with software vendors. Other approaches to community vulnerability discovery include the Pwn2Own contest at CanSecWest, and organized crowdsourced security testing from companies like Bugcrowd and Synack.

Game Theory for Malware Analysis

Cybersecurity involves interactions between attackers and defenders, and it is effected by the probability of a system being attacked. This interaction can be described in terms of a game. Game theory is the study and mathematical modeling of decision-making which took its name in the 1940s and soon spread from economics to biology and later computer science. The "games" that we study could be chess or blackjack, but are just as useful to cyber-related topics such as peer-to-peer file sharing, online advertising auctions, and computer hackers. The games are represented by mathematical models that describe the players, the actions available to the players, payoffs of actions, and information. Players use strategies to pick actions based on information in order to maximize payoffs.

The execution of game theory goes something like this. Each player makes moves from a set of available moves and follows constraints established for the game. Players have an information set—knowledge of different variables at a particular point in time. Players also have a strategy, which is a rule that tells the player what action to take at each instance of the game, given her information set. The outcome is the set of interesting elements that arise due to selections that you, the modeler, pick for values of the information, actions, payoffs, and other variables after the game is played out.

Why would game theory be useful to you if the approach is largely theoretical? Here is one example to help illustrate the answer. Say you manage security for a startup video streaming company. You need to figure out how many servers to deploy around the globe with the assumption that these servers are likely to be attacked. Modeling the interaction between your company and adversaries can shed light on the number of servers required.

Game Theory for Security Resource Allocation

Game theory is well suited to security resource allocation and scheduling problems. Algorithms for solving Bayesian Stackelberg games are used in a variety of real-world applications:

- ARMOR (Assistant for Randomized Monitoring over Routes) has been used at the Los Angeles International Airport to randomize roadway checkpoints and terminal patrol routes.

- IRIS (Intelligent Randomization in Scheduling) is a game-theoretic scheduler for randomized deployment of the US Federal Air Marshals.

- PROTECT (Port Resilience Operational/Tactical Enforcement to Combat Terrorism) has been used for randomizing US Coast Guard patrolling.

- GUARDS (Game-Theoretic Unpredictable and Randomly Deployed Security) has been used to aid the US Transportation Security Administration in scheduling resources to protect airports.

- TRUSTS (Tactical Randomization for Urban Security in Transit Systems) has been used in some urban transit systems to compute optimal patrol strategies.

Game theory has an interesting solution concept called the Nash equilibrium, named for mathematician John Forbes Nash, Jr. (subject of the movie *A Beautiful Mind*). The Nash equilibrium describes a state in game theory where the optimal outcome of a game is one where no player has an incentive to deviate from his or her chosen strategy after considering an opponent's choice. Mutually assured destruction is a form of the Nash equilibrium where the use of a weapon would destroy both sides.

Honeypots are realistic-looking decoy systems that network defenders use to lure attackers. The honeypot allows a defender to observe and monitor attackers' activities in a controlled environment, thus informing the defender about how to better defend his or her environment.

Several years ago, a team of researchers studied how honeypots could best be used to deceive potential attackers.[1] Network administrators were familiar with the benefits of honeypots, but were simply guessing about the number and location of where to place them in the network to maximize network defense. You can imagine that malware analysts, on the other hand, might be interested in figuring out where to place honeypots that would be more likely to attract malware and generate data to aid malware analysis. In Figure 9-1, you can see one result from the researchers' report showing that the Nash equilibrium strategy significantly outperforms the baseline strategies. Game theory also allowed these researchers to show that the optimal strategy for honeypots is randomized and distributed throughout the network, not always masquerading as the most or least valuable machines in the network.

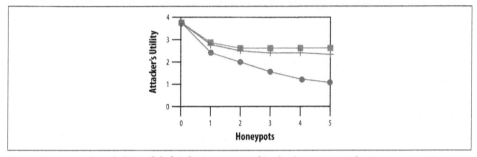

Figure 9-1. Exploitability of defender strategies for the honeypot selection game; Xs = Nash Equilibrium, Squares = Maximum, Pluses = Random

Compare the Nash equilibrium to a cat-and-mouse game, which is the langauge often used to describe the relationship between attackers and defenders in cybersecurity. We tend to think of cybersecurity as having no equilibrium, but rather being a game of constant pursuit. Both attackers and defenders in cybersecurity can improve their situation by changing actions. Moving target defense (described in Chapter 10) is such a situation.

Another technique in game theory is called Stackelberg games. Stackelberg security games are attacker-defender games where the defender attempts to allocate limited resources to protect a set of targets, and the adversary plans to attack one such target. In these games, the defender first commits to a strategy assuming that the adversary can observe that strategy. Then, the adversary takes his response after seeing the defender's strategy. This is perhaps a stronger claim than reality, where defenders may face uncertainty about the attacker's ability to observe the defense strategy.

---

1 Radek Píbil, Viliam Lisy, Christopher Kiekintveld, Branislav Bosansky, and Michal Pechoucek. "Game Theoretic Model of Strategic Honeypot Allocation in Computer Networks," In: *Decision and Game Theory for Security*. Conference on Decision and Game Theory for Security, Budapest, 2012-11-05/2012-11-06. Heidelberg: Springer-Verlag, GmbH, 2012, pp. 201–220. Lecture Notes in Computer Science. vol. 7638. 2012.

Game theory has some strong limitations to consider. First, players in real-life versions of a game are not as rational as a game suggests. Second, in most practical settings, the costs and motivations of other players is uncertain and difficult to determine. Third, game theory often ignores human components of real-life decisions such as the regret (or fear of regret) of poor decisions.

You can run game theory scientific experiments with mathematical software including Mathematica and Maple, or with free software such as Gambit (*http://gambit.sour ceforge.net*) and Gams (*http://www.gams.com*). These software packages allow you to run the games described above, including Stackelberg security games.

Case Study: Identifying Malware Families with Science

In this section, we consider a hypothetical scientific experiment for a method of categorizing malware binaries into families. We first look at similar work that others have done on the topic to differentiate this experiment from that other work. Then, we describe how one might run a new experiment.

Building on Previous Work

From 2010–2014, DARPA ran a research program called Cyber Genome. The project was designed to determine whether there were discernible "fingerprints" of malware authors in malware binaries. Another goal was to study the ability to detect malware genealogy and construct "family trees" using similarity metrics. Some companies who participated in the research went on to create commercial products including Cynomix, a cloud-based "patent-pending cyber genome analysis technology" from Invincea (*http://www.invincea.com/products/cynomix/*).

Having heard about DARPA's research, assume that you want to write a program to automatically determine whether you have seen a similar variant of a piece of malware before. This technique is similar to using biological DNA profiling to identify evidence of a genetic relationship. This feature might be useful in an antivirus product or network security appliance where you could tell users "we haven't seen this file before, but it appears similar to Trojan X."

In 2009, researchers building algorithms for determining malware relationships constructed the image in Figure 9-2 to illustrate the biggest of 14 families of Bagle malware in their dataset. The research team also tested their algorithms with the Mytob malware family, which show relations between the Mydoom, Polybot, and Gaobot malware.

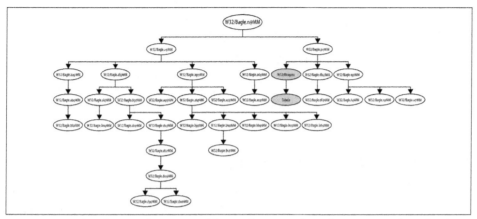

Figure 9-2. A family tree of variants of the Bagle worm, from "An Empirical Study of Malware Evolution" (2009)

Biological DNA profiling was first reported in 1985 by Sir Alec Jeffreys. The first criminal conviction to use DNA evidence in the US occurred two years later. To date, no criminal cases have been decided using malware fingerprinting.

A New Experiment

You have a novel algorithm for cyber DNA profiling that you think can match new, never-before-seen malware samples with digital relatives in a known set. You want to offer proof of this claim, and embark on experimentation to evaluate this hypothesis:

> My cyber DNA profiling algorithm can correctly identify digital genetic relationships of new samples with known malware families with 95% confidence.

One approach to testing this hypothesis is to simply try malware samples and see how well your algorithm works. A key challenge with this kind of testing, however, is that you have to know ground truth to determine whether or not the algorithm performed correctly. During the testing, you essentially need to know the answer about which malware family the test sample belongs to before you start. Even if you are successful in this regard, perhaps by using known variants of malware as the researchers did with Mytob and Bagle, people may be unconvinced by your results.

Ground truth malware sets for testing are a challenge for everyone building malware solutions. One research team doing malware clustering in 2009 chose to use 2,658 samples (from a set of 14,212) that a majority of six antivirus programs agreed upon. In 2013, students at the Naval Postgraduate School manually created a small dataset of ground truth malware for their Ground Truth Malware Database. Malware samples with and without labels can be obtained for free from various websites, including

Contagio Malware Dump (*http://contagiodump.blogspot.com*), Open Malware (*http://openmalware.org*), and VirusShare (*http://virusshare.com*).

The sample size required for this experiment is impossible to estimate because there is no way to accurately determine whether you have a representative sample of all malware. People are likely to question your results if you use a sample size that they consider too small. In general, aim for hundreds or thousands of samples whenever possible.

How to Find More Information

Advances and scientific results in malware analysis are shared at cybersecurity and topic-specific workshops and conferences. REcon is one annual reverse engineering conference. Virus Bulletin hosts an annual international conference on malware and other cyber threats. The IEEE International Conference on Malicious and Unwanted Software (MALCON) presents theoretical and applied knowledge of malware-related tools, practices, and incidents. The Conference on Decision and Game Theory for Security (GameSec) is one forum for academic and industrial researchers in game theory and technological systems.

Conclusion

This chapter presented the application of cybersecurity science to malware analysis. The key takeaways are:

- Malware analysis tools are enabled and improved through science. Security researchers conduct experiments that produce practical advances in tools and techniques for malware analysis, in knowing how malware spreads, and how to deter and mitigate the threat.

- Malware analysis simulators and sandboxes sometimes have features that support the scientific method, including reproducible execution, reliable data collection, and virtual machine introspection.

- Game theory is one way to practice cybersecurity science, analyzing interactions between attackers and defenders as a strategic game.

- We applied the scientific method to malware analysis using a hypothetical case to study the ability to identify relationships between similar malware binaries.

References

- Matthew O. Jackson. "A Brief Introduction to the Basics of Game Theory" (*http://papers.ssrn.com/sol3/papers.cfm?abstract_id=1968579*) (2011)

- Michael Sikorski and Andrew Honig. *Practical Malware Analysis* (San Francisco, CA: No Starch Press, 2012)

- Steven Tadelis. *Game Theory: An Introduction* (Princeton, NJ: Princeton University Press, 2013)

## CHAPTER 10

System Security Engineering

I once heard that Yahoo has full-time employees who are responsible for replacing failed hard drives in its 50,000+ servers. If the average hard drive lasts for two years, then Yahoo has to replace roughly 69 hard drives per day! System security engineering in cybersecurity is about building and evaluating systems to be dependable in the face of adversaries and errors. Building a secure system is ideally about taking an unambiguous policy, formally validating the hardware design and implementation, formally validating the software, and generating scads of documentation. Such a system, despite precise, formalized elegance, is not usable. Therefore, we have to compromise on pieces of this idealized development and engineering process. For every compromise there comes some risk, and the security engineer must try to drive down that risk, recognizing that it can never reach zero. Science can help you analyze the options and figure out how to mitigate them.

Understanding security requirements at the system level—the big picture—requires cross-disciplinary skills and tools. Security engineers should consider economics, psychology, and ethics in addition to information technology. Examples of broad systems of this nature include enterprise networks, electronic voting solutions, and online web services. You probably don't have to think about system security for anything the size of Facebook, but the principles of system-level security are just as important for basic client-server applications and small business computer networks. As a system-level risk, security engineering takes on different kinds of scientific experimentation. In this chapter, we will look at those differences. You will also learn the powerful analysis technique of regression analysis, how to evaluate system security through the lens of moving target defense, and a walk-through experiment to defend against unintentional insider threats.

Scientific experimentation should not be an answer to the statement "I don't know how to design a system." Instead, science in this domain is useful for testing hypotheses about how the system will react and for helping to measure the security impact of your engineering choices, and therefore provides insights about how to improve system-level security. Say you are responsible for deploying public key infrastructure (PKI) in your enterprise. As the infosec professional, you should understand, test, and document what attackers could do from various vantage points in your network such as man-in-the-middle attacks or phishing, how you could effectively monitor the PKI deployment, and how human users might affect the system in situations like high load.

There are many research questions in security engineering that apply to new and existing solutions. You may ask specific questions, like "does this system maintain its integrity under specific stressors?" Well-designed experiments can answer such questions. You may also ask, "does the composition of components increase the attack surface of the system?" You could certainly design experiments that launch a suite of attacks against the system and measure the system's response. You may want to help answer questions that nobody has solved to date, like how to measure attack surfaces using experimentation.

The research problems in system security engineering are both technical and non-technical. For example, it is difficult to manage evaluations because tools for measuring security protections for different parts of the system are so different. Measurements of security in cryptographic algorithms cannot be easily compared to measurements of security in human usability. How could we improve the Common Criteria, which many regard as pointlessly bureaucratic? Research is needed to make these evaluations compatible and cohesive. Other disciplines, such as economics, have tools for understanding risk even with incomplete information. Cybersecurity still has much to learn from these other disciplines.

Cybersecurity Models, Principles, and Theories: Hypotheses in Disguise

An awful lot of traditional cybersecurity—formal models, design principles, theories —are really hypotheses in disguise. Sometimes these are the result of thorough investigation and scientific scrutiny, but many haven't been subjected to a lot of rigorous analysis, despite the fact that they are widely taught. In Chapter 1 we said that there are few axioms in security, but in reality we too often take our models, principles, and theories as axiomatic without realizing it.

For just one example, consider Saltzer's and Schroeder's Design Principles from their paper The Protection of Information in Computer Systems.[1] One blogger called this

---

1 J. H. Saltzer and M. D. Schroeder. "The protection of information in computer systems," *Proceedings of the IEEE*, vol. 63, no. 9, pp. 1278–1308, Sept. 1975.

paper "one of the most cited, least read works in computer security history." The principles proposed by Saltzer and Schroeder, shown below, were added to textbooks and influenced the DoD's *Trusted Computer System Evaluation Criteria*. Over time the principles solidified into guidelines. Look over the list and think about ways you could test them as hypotheses. The bottom line is that you should proceed cautiously before taking anything as sacrosanct, even long-standing models, principles, and theories.

- Principle of Economy of Mechanism
- Principle of Fail-Safe Defaults
- Principle of Complete Mediation
- Principle of Open Design
- Principle of Separation of Privilege
- Principle of Least Privilege
- Principle of Least Common Mechanism
- Principle of Psychological Acceptability

An Example Scientific Experiment in System Security Engineering

For an example of scientific experimentation in system engineering, see the paper "An Epidemiological Study of Malware Encounters in a Large Enterprise" by Yen et al.[2] In the abstract below you can see that this study attempted to answer research questions about patterns of malware encounters, including "How did the malware infiltrate network perimeter?" and "Can we predict which users will encounter malware?" Elsewhere in the paper we learn that the authors analyzed McAfee antivirus logs from 85,000+ hosts in a multinational enterprise over four months. Among the findings were that malware rates varied widely across countries, that employees were three times more likely to be infected outside the enterprise network (e.g., at home), and that malware encounters were highest among people with technical jobs. Using regression (described in "Regression Analysis" on page 115), the researchers built a classifier (an algorithm that maps input to a category) that could successfully identify hosts at high risk for malware. Note that this study used the epidemiological method —the science of patterns, causes, and effects (often of medical diseases)—and that there was no stated hypothesis or controlled experiment.

---

2 T. Yen, V. Heorhiadi, A. Oprea, M. Reiter, A. Juels. "An Epidemiological Study of Malware Encounters in a Large Enterprise." In *ACM Conference on Computer and Communications Security*, 2014.

Abstract from a system security engineering experiment

We present an epidemiological study of malware encounters in a large, multinational enterprise. Our datasets allow us to observe or infer not only malware presence on enterprise computers, but also malware entry points, network locations of the computers (i.e., inside the enterprise network or outside) when the malware were encountered, and for some web-based malware encounters, web activities that gave rise to them. By coupling this data with demographic information for each host's primary user, such as his or her job title and level in the management hierarchy, we are able to paint a reasonably comprehensive picture of malware encounters for this enterprise. We use this analysis to build a logistic regression model for inferring the risk of hosts encountering malware; those ranked highly by our model have a greater than three times higher rate of encountering malware than the base rate. We also discuss where our study confirms or refutes other studies and guidance that our results suggest.

Science and Artifacts

You may encounter fellow developers, engineers, scientists, and infosec professionals who believe that artifacts are not contributions to science. When people do experiments and studies and the end result is a piece of software or hardware, that result is called an *artifact*. The experimental result and product stem from human activity and not of a natural phenomenon under investigation. Artifacts are not well respected in terms of their scientific content, sometimes unfairly. In discussing whether or not his own study was "science" or not, one co-author of the preceding abstract summarized their contribution as "[a] classifier for prioritizing responses to infection indicators… that's an artifact!" However, the software is essential to illustrating what has been accomplished, in the same way that a visualization program illustrates the scientific results and developments behind it. Think of proof-of-concept artifacts as a way to show the properties claimed for a new methodology; you use the methodology to produce an implementation, and others can assess both the methodology and the artifact.

Let's look at how you could conduct a study in your own network similar to the epidemiological study above. Your hypothesis could be that people with the title "Vice President" have a higher rate of infection. Here's an approach:

1. Gather antivirus alerts for the enterprise. If you run McAfee ePolicy Orchestrator, export the Threat Event Log by querying the EPOEvents table and exporting as a CSV file named *infections.csv*. Here is a query to select the victim's hostname, username, IP address, threat name (e.g., W32/Conficker.worm), and threat type (e.g., "worm").

   ```
   SELECT [TargetHostName], [TargetUserName],
   dbo.RSDFN_ConvertIntToIPString (TargetIPV4), [ThreatName]
   [ThreatType] FROM [dbo].[EPOEvents]
   ```

You should get a CSV file with contents like this:

```
workstation5,dykstra,10.5.1.4,W32/Conficker.worm,Worm
workstation5,dykstra,10.5.1.4,Downloader.gen.a,Trojan
workstation32,smith,10.17.0.2,W32/Conficker.worm,Worm
...
```

2. Gather usernames and titles. In Active Directory for Windows, you can retrieve all accounts and save them to *username_titles.csv* with this PowerShell command:

```
get-aduser -SizeLimit 0 -Properties Title,SamAccountName \
|Export-Csv username_titles.csv
```

You should get a CSV file with contents like this:

```
Senior Researcher,dykstra
CEO,smith
Programmer,alice
...
```

3. Now combine the two files based on common usernames. In Linux, use this command:

```
# Compare the usernames: 2nd field in username_titles.csv and 2nd field
#     in infections.csv
# If there's a match, print the second field in username_titles.csv
#     (SamAccountName) and the fifth field in infections.csv (ThreatType)

awk 'NR==FNR{username_titles[$2]=$1;next}{print username_titles[$2]",\
            "$5;}' FS="," username_titles.csv infections.csv
```

You should get output like this:

```
Senior Researcher,Worm
Senior Researcher,Trojan
CEO,Worm
...
```

You could extend this example using IP addresses to compare infections inside the enterprise network to those outside. In the next section, we will learn how to do regression analysis, which you could also apply to this example.

Regression Analysis

Regression analysis is one of the most widely used data analysis techniques for estimating the relationships among variables. In particular, regression is used to predict the future values of the dependent variable. Regression is a mathematical model represented by equations, and exact relationships do not exist in regression analysis. There are many types of regression analysis that differ in the types of variables used in the equations of the model. You are most likely to encounter *linear regression*, which uses one independent variable to explain or predict the outcome of one dependent variable. The relationship between the variables is typically in the form of a straight "best fit" line (for linear regression) that best approximates all the individual data points. Regression analysis is a very broad and complex topic only skimmed here to let you understand the basic concept.

 The formula for converting between Fahrenheit and Celsius is an exact relationship (F = (9/5)C + 32). Unlike regression, the relationship is known exactly so there is no need to model the relationship.

British statistician George Box famously said that "essentially, all models are wrong, but some are useful."[3] The truth in this statement comes from the fact that models are simplifications and approximations of reality that often ignore important factors (e.g., friction, gravity, etc.). However, models are still useful for understanding our complex world and making predictions. Regression analysis is useful in practical cybersecurity because predictions can inform our choices about how to build, deploy, or configure cybersecurity solutions.

Statistical software such as MATLAB and R make regression analysis approachable for nonexperts. The output of the software will include coefficients for the regression equation. The strength of the model is expressed in these correlation coefficients, which explain how much of the predicted value can be explained by the regression formula. Generally ranging from 0 to 1, a value of 0 indicates no predictive power, 0.1–0.3 weak prediction, 0.4–0.6 moderate prediction, and 0.7–1 strong prediction. The following example has a correlation of 0.68, or moderate predictive ability. Purely scientific studies often strive for values of .9 or above, but 0.68 may be good enough to influence the system design.

Suppose you were developing a cloud-based smartphone security app and wanted to know how to balance battery consumption with your app's activity on the device. Your hypothesis is that bandwidth usage is a significant factor correlated with battery usage. You collect some sample data from people similar to your target audience, like that in Table 10-1.

You can graph the data in R using the lm (linear model) and plot commands, along with a "best fit" line, as follows (see Figure 10-1):

```
# Load the data from a CSV file
mydata <- read.csv("data.txt", header=TRUE)

# Create a scatterplot of bandwidth versus battery discharge
plot(mydata$bandwidth,mydata$battery)
```

---

3 George E. P. Box and Norman R. Draper. *Empirical Model-Building and Response Surfaces* (Wiley, 1987).

```
# Calculate the coefficients of regression model
fit <- lm(mydata$battery~mydata$bandwidth)

# Use the coefficients to draw the Line of Best Fit
abline(fit)
```

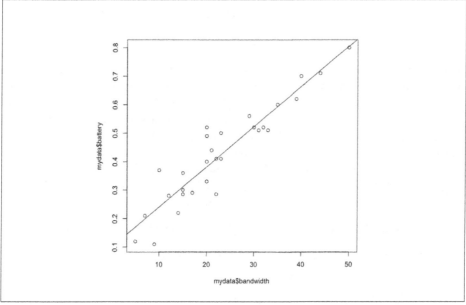

Figure 10-1. Regression scatterplot of actual battery/bandwidth values and the Line of Best Fit showing the calculated approximate values from the regression model

You also want to test that other factors (CPU utilization, WiFi state, I/O idle rate) are not as significantly correlated with battery usage. The `cor` command calculates the correlations between all variable pairs as follows:

```
# Compute the correlation coefficient between bandwidth and battery discharge
> cor(mydata$bandwidth,mydata$battery)
[1] 0.681595

# Compute a correlation matrix for all variables
> cor(mydata)
                CPU        wifi          IO    bandwidth      battery
CPU      1.00000000 -0.4373735  0.65467277   0.36014650   0.08320651
wifi    -0.43737346  1.0000000 -0.80266372   0.28494970   0.22539850
IO       0.65467277 -0.8026637  1.00000000  -0.04450642  -0.15041226
bandwidth 0.36014650  0.2849497 -0.04450642   1.00000000   0.68159530
battery  0.08320651  0.2253985 -0.15041226   0.68159530   1.00000000
```

Table 10-1. An example data excerpt of smartphone attributes and battery discharge

cpu_utilization (%)	wifi_state (on, off)	io_idle (%)	bandwidth (kb/s)	battery_discharge
0.2	0	0.008	0	0.36
0.3	1	0.001	20	0.52
0.1	0	0.17	10	0.37
0.2	1	0.06	20	0.40
0.4	1	0	100	0.66

After the regression analysis is complete, *cross-validation* is used to check the model by assessing how the results will generalize to an independent dataset. This is necessary because models sometimes incorrectly estimate how accurately a predictive model will perform in practice. Cross-validation is performed in rounds, where each round consists of partitioning a dataset into subsets, performing the analysis on one subset (the *training set*), and validating the analysis on the other subset (the *validation set*). Ten-fold cross-validation is common, where the data is partitioned into 10 subsets, cross-validation is performed 10 times, and in each round nine samples are used for the training set and one sample is used as the validation set.

You can perform 10-fold cross-validation in R using the DAAG package as follows:

```
# 10-Fold Cross-Validation for Linear Regression
# df = a data frame
# m = number of folds (rounds)
library(DAAG)
cv.lm(df=mydata, fit, m=10)
```

As you can see, regression is a complicated topic but becomes easier to do with modern tools. It is an important and powerful concept that plays a part in many scientific discoveries. As you consider your own cybersecurity experiments, remember that regression can help analyze the relationships among variables.

Moving Target Defense

In a blog post several years ago, Netflix revealed that it had a Chaos Monkey (*http://techblog.netflix.com/2011/07/netflix-simian-army.html*).[4] The Netflix infrastructure runs in the cloud, and the Chaos Monkey was a program that terminated random virtual machine instances in its infrastructure. Why? Because it believed that "the best defense against major unexpected failures is to fail often." By failing often, Netflix forces its applications to be resilient to the chaos.

---

4 See also, the Chaos Monkey source code (*http://techblog.netflix.com/2012/07/chaos-monkey-released-into-wild.html*).

Moving Target Defense (MTD) is the concept of routine change in a system or environment to increase uncertainty and apparent complexity for potential attackers. It can also reduce attackers' window of opportunity and increase the costs of their attack efforts because, from their perspective, their targets change "randomly" over time. MTD is typically used for Internet-facing hosts rather than internal to a network, but this is not required. Examples of MTD include network configuration randomization and address space randomization. Many IT environments today remain static for years, giving adversaries time to learn and attack the system. For example, your web server may have been at the same IP address running the same version of Apache for many years. MTD introduces the element of surprise, such as changing the web server's IP address in an unpredictable way. Chaos Monkey is an example of MTD because a virtual machine could be terminated at any time.

MTD makes the bold assumption that perfect security is unattainable in practice. Given that starting point, and the assumption that all systems are compromised, MTD focuses on enabling the continued safe operation in a compromised environment and having systems that are defensible rather than perfectly secure. As a complex system, MTD offers an opportunity for cybersecurity science. There are interesting hypotheses to test in selecting and deploying moving target defenses in your environment. Does the use of diversity limit spreading attacks? Is there any measurable difference in spread rates when using static environments versus dynamic diversity? What experiments would you want to run to convince your management that MTD was a wise choice?

One cost of deploying MTD is the overhead of managing and executing the moves, making complex systems intentionally more complex. Not only must the system itself be able to implement regular changes, but so must those who interact with that system. If you change the IP address of your web server every day, the network defense team and intrusion detection systems must be aware of what the current, legitimate IP address is at any given time. Decision-makers appreciate analysis that shows that the anticipated cost and risk of not deploying MTD are greater than the anticipated cost and risk of adopting and implementing a change.

Risk assessments tend to evaluate the environment at a single moment in time. As a result, they would fail to adequately capture the risk of a static target over time, or the benefit of change. Think back to earlier in the chapter about the algorithm to predict which machines in an enterprise were likely to encounter malware. Now think like an attacker: if the attacker knows that you have some way to predict the vulnerable users or machines, she will try to fool your algorithm and attack users or machines that break the algorithm's regular rules. In this common attacker-defender cat-and-mouse game, you can imagine that changing even one variable in the environment could lower the risk of an otherwise vulnerable machine: changing machine IP addresses, deploying different web browsers, or randomly running full-disk malware scans on machines that return to the enterprise after connecting remotely. A well-designed experiment studying a small pilot MTD deployment would let you measure whether or not users encounter more or less malware after implementing MTD.

Case Study: Defending Against Unintentional Insider Threats

In this section, we will walk through a hypothetical scientific experiment related to one important aspect of system security engineering: insider threats. This experiment explores the risk of unintentional insider threat in a corporate setting. Though they can be just as damaging as intentional insiders who deliberately and maliciously intend to cause harm, unintentional insiders are those employees who accidentally or inadvertently expose the business to risk, often without even knowing it.

 Insider threat is a widely acknowledged and serious security concern for many businesses. The CERT Insider Threat Center at Carnegie Mellon University has been studying the topic, and released a report in 2013 describing "unintentional insider threat" as insider actions or inactions *without malicious intent* which cause harm or increase the probability of harm.[5]

The goal of this experiment is to determine if unintentional insiders could harm your particular enterprise, and make the case for specific remediations to better protect the network. Say you work at a financial services company with 500 employees spread across three locations: Boston, Denver, and Tokyo. The company handles sensitive financial information and any data breaches would cause significant harm to clients and your company. You don't know how often unprotected sensitive information leaves the company on employee devices, so you're interested in whether data loss prevention (DLP) technology could help mitigate this risk. You form a hypothesis as follows:

> Data loss prevention software would protect the enterprise by discovering 90% of outgoing email messages containing unprotected sensitive company data.

This hypothesis is a bit different from some other case studies that were presented. The hypothesis seeks to understand the benefit of taking an action: adding DLP to the environment. The tests will help demonstrate whether this action will result in the hypothesized outcomes. This is clearly a very narrow, technology-focused question that ignores the benefits of other mitigations to insider threat, including complementary approaches such as user education and awareness.

---

5 CERT Insider Threat Team. *Unintentional Insider Threats: A Foundational Study* (*http://resources.sei.cmu.edu/library/asset-view.cfm?assetID=58744*). Software Engineering Institute, May 2013

"One size fits all" approaches to insider threats may be inappropriate even inside a single company or organization. For example, you may wish to tailor solutions to certain individuals or business units such as stock traders in a financial services company. High risk tolerance is desirable and valued in some circumstances, so insider threat education and awareness strategies should avoid inappropriately stifling the employees in those circumstances.

To measure the benefit of DLP, you will need a control group of users who do not use it. However, you will need ground-truth data about what sensitive information those users are storing and transmitting that might have been identified by DLP. There are at least three options: construct an artificial emulated environment where you monitor simulated real-world activity, use questionnaires with a representative sample of real-world employees of self-reported activity, or review users' real-world activity yourself (e.g., looking at email on the mail server—with or without their knowledge). Assume you pick the last option, to review the email of 10 users on the mail server for one week without notifying them.[6] You discover that 30% of messages contain sensitive company data.

Now you want to evaluate a commercial DLP solution. After installing and configuring the software to detect your sensitive information, you need to gather data. As with the control group, you have choices about where and how to collect data. In this case, it would be wise to measure how the DLP software works for the same users and same email data as you manually examined. This approach enables you to definitively identify true positives (DLP correctly identified sensitive data), false positives (DLP incorrectly identified sensitive data), and false negatives (DLP missed sensitive data). At the end of the week, you find that DLP found that 28% of messages contained sensitive company data, with 2% false negatives and 0% false positives. Clearly, you have confirmed the hypothesis that DLP can discover 90% of the sensitive data in email for this small sample.

Note that we have detected sensitive data in outgoing email but we have not determined whether the sender's intent was malicious or an unintentional risk. Intent is difficult to measure. While you could alert the email sender that his message contains sensitive data and ask him if he wants to proceed, this is unlikely to dissuade malicious insiders. Some DLP solutions allow you to automatically route emails with sensitive data to an email gateway that will automatically encrypt the message. You may be able to construct a follow-on experiment that measures the percentage of messages violating a policy of only sending encrypted emails to known, verified recipients.

---

6 Of course, this action is legal and consistent with the "Consent to Monitor" clause in your Employee Handbook, and approved by management and legal counsel.

How to Find More Information

Scientific results in security engineering appear in all kinds of cybersecurity solutions, even if they remain hidden from most users. A recent job opening at Google for Information Security Engineer included the responsibility to "conduct research to identify new attack vectors against Google's products and services" and one for a Product Security Engineer at Facebook said: "You will be relied upon to provide engineering and product teams with the security expertise necessary to make confident product decisions. Come help us make life hard for the bad guys." Advances and scientific results are shared with the public at conferences such as the IEEE/IFIP International Conference on Dependable Systems and Networks (DSN) and the Network and Distributed System Security Symposium (NDSS). There is an annual Workshop on Moving Target Defense in conjunction with the ACM Conference on Computer and Communications Security (CCS).

Conclusion

System security engineering requires cybersecurity science that uses cross-disciplinary skills and tools. The key concepts and takeaways from this chapter are:

- Science in this domain is useful for testing hypotheses about how the system will react and for helping to measure the security impact of your engineering choices, providing insights about how to improve system-level security.

- Regression analysis is a widely used data analysis technique for estimating the relationships among variables. Regression is used to predict the future values of the dependent variable.

- Moving target defense is a concept of routine change in a system or environment to reduce attackers' window of opportunity because, from their perspective, their targets change "randomly" over time.

- In a hypothetical case study, we evaluated the hypothesis that data loss prevention software would protect an enterprise by discovering outgoing email messages containing sensitive company data.

References

- ACM Workshop on Moving Target Defense (*http://mtd.mobicloud.asu.edu*)
- Ross Anderson. *Security Engineering: A Guide to Building Dependable Distributed Systems* (Indianapolis, IN: Wiley, 2008)
- Richard Cook. *How Complex Systems Fail* (*http://web.mit.edu/2.75/resources/random/How%20Complex%20Systems%20Fail.pdf*) (1998)

- John Fox and Sanford Weisberg. *An R Companion to Applied Regression, Second Edition* (Thousand Oaks, CA: Sage, 2011)

- Jay Jacobs and Bob Rudis. *Data-Driven Security: Analysis, Visualization and Dashboards* (Indianapolis, IN: Wiley, 2014)

- Thomas P. Ryan. *Modern Regression Methods*, 2nd Edition (Indianapolis, IN: Wiley, 2009)

- Adam Shostack. *Threat Modeling: Designing for Security* (Indianapolis, IN: Wiley, 2014)

## CHAPTER 11

Human-Computer Interaction and Usable Security

Usability affects many cybersecurity domains presented throughout this book. Like other cybersecurity issues, human-computer interaction and usable security also rely on empirical experimentation. Good work in these areas also requires an understanding of how humans work. Despite its widespread applicability, usability evaluation is often overlooked and undervalued. In this chapter you will learn about the scientific principle of double-blind experimentation, how to measure usability during design and validation, and how to evaluate the usability of a cybersecurity product.

In "A Roadmap for Cybersecurity Research" published by DHS in 2009, usable security is identified as one of 11 hard problems in infosec research. This report, and others like it, point out that security and usability have historically been at odds. This situation comes in part from implementation choices that make security choices unintuitive and confusing. Security adds complexity to a system and interferes with the user's primary goals, so it is an area where collaboration between the cybersecurity community and the usability research community is required. The science of usability as applied to security is an unmet goal.

Usability is important to consumers, as evidenced by online product reviews. For example, Qihoo 360 Security - Antivirus Free (for Android) received this review (*http://www.pcmag.com/article2/0,2817,2468630,00.asp*) from PC Magazine:

> "...I felt overwhelmed by the sheer number of features, and was disappointed when several of them didn't work as advertised (or at all). And the app doesn't do a great job of explaining itself, or making some of its most critical features—like anti-theft tools— easy to use."

Experimentation and testing in human-computer interaction and usable security are naturally more difficult to automate and scale than some other problems we've explored in the book. When Ford wants to test a new engine part, it can use well-designed models and simulations to run 20,000 tests with the push of a button and very little cost. When it wants to test dashboards, it's not so easy to know what consumers are going to like without doing user studies.

Usability for cybersecurity differs from general usability in several ways. For one, security is often not the primary task or concern for users. Adding security features to an email client, for example, disrupts the primary goal of sending and receiving email. Another uniqueness to usable security is the adversary. An adversary might try to take advantage of the features or flaws in human-computer interfaces and usability, even using social engineering to persuade the user into compromising security. Research topics in human-computer interaction (HCI) and usable security evolve over time as computer interaction changes. Usability of wearable technology such as fitness trackers differs from usability of a traditional laptop computer.[1]

An Example Scientific Experiment in Usable Security

Experiments in design and usability follow a variation on our familiar formula: participants (evaluators and users), evaluation procedure, and the environment and system setup. One kind of experiment is usability testing, completing specific tasks in a controlled manner. Another kind of experiment requires users to responding to specific questions. Yet another compares alternative designs, perhaps using analytical modeling and simulation. In his classic handbook on usability, *Usability Engineering*, Jakob Nielsen recommends that you conduct pilot runs during this phase, especially if user involvement is required.

Recall from Chapter 3 that there are important choices about where to conduct an experiment. In human factors, the setting can be especially important if it influences the participants. A 2011 study experimentally showed a difference between self-reported and observed actions related to web browser SSL warnings. The authors reported that "...one third of our participants claimed that their reaction would be different if they were not in a study environment and did not have the reassurance from the study environment (e.g., ethics board approval, the university as a reputable organization) that their information would be safe and secure."[2]

For an example of scientific experimentation in usability, look at the paper "Does My Password Go Up to Eleven? The Impact of Password Meters on Password Selection"

---

1 For more, see National Research Council Steering Committee on the Usability, Security, and Privacy of Computer Systems, *Toward Better Usability, Security, and Privacy of Information Technology: A Report of a Workshop*. Washington, DC: The National Academies Press, 2010.

2 Andreas Sotirakopoulos, Kirstie Hawkey, and Konstantin Beznosov. *On the Challenges in Usable Security Lab Studies: Lessons Learned from Replicating a Study on SSL Warnings* (Proceedings of the Seventh Symposium on Usable Privacy and Security (SOUPS), 2011).

by Egelman et al. (2013).[3] In the abstract below you can see that this study involved both a laboratory experiment and field experiment. The stated hypotheses (presented later in the paper) for the laboratory experiment were:

H_0

> Passwords are not stronger when meters are present.

H_1

> Passwords are stronger when users see relative strength meters compared to no meters.

H_2

> Passwords are stronger when users see relative strength meters compared to "traditional" meters.

The stated hypotheses for the field experiment, based on data collected in the laboratory, were:

H_{0a}

> Passwords are not stronger when users see meters, when creating unimportant accounts.

H_{0b}

> Changes to the orientation and text of password meters will not result in different passwords.

Abstract from a human factors experiment

Password meters tell users whether their passwords are "weak" or "strong." We performed a laboratory experiment to examine whether these meters influenced users' password selections when they were forced to change their real passwords, and when they were not told that their passwords were the subject of a study. We observed that the presence of meters yielded significantly stronger passwords. We performed a followup field experiment to test a different scenario: creating a password for an unimportant account. In this scenario, we found that the meters made no observable difference: participants simply reused weak passwords that they used to protect similar low-risk accounts. We conclude that meters result in stronger passwords when users are forced to change existing passwords on "important" accounts and that individual meter design decisions likely have a marginal impact.

---

3 Serge Egelman, Andreas Sotirakopoulos, Ildar Muslukhov, Konstantin Beznosov, and Cormac Herley. 2013. Does my password go up to eleven?: The impact of password meters on password selection. In Proceedings of the SIGCHI Conference on Human Factors in Computing Systems (CHI '13). ACM, New York, NY.

This would be a straightforward experiment for you to replicate. The most challenging part of this study is the experimental design: how do you get study participants to think that the thing you're measuring (passwords) isn't the subject of the study?

Five Myths of Usability

The website UX Myths (*http://uxmyths.com*) collects frequent misconceptions about design and usability. Here are five such misconceptions based on their collection that are useful for security usability:

1. **You are like your users.** As a designer or developer, you know and care about your product or service more than your users. To avoid your own bias, learn about and interact with your users, and involve them in the development process.

2. **Users make optimal choices.** Usability tests show that users tend to choose the first somewhat reasonable choice that catches their eye, instead of selecting the optimal choice.

3. **People can tell you what they want.** Users routinely have difficulty articulating what they want in a product. They also make confident but false predictions about their future behavior. This is related to another myth: usability is about asking users what they want.

4. **Usability testing is expensive.** Getting user input should be disciplined and systematic but can be fast and relatively cheap. Just remember, usability testing is not the same as asking a few friends if they like your product. Done right and early in the development process, usability doesn't have to slow down development.

5. **If you are an expert, you don't need to test your design.** Usability testing and expert reviews are both useful but tend to reveal different issues.

Double-Blind Experimentation

Blind experimentation describes a type of experimental procedure where information is concealed from the test subject or the experimenter to avoid human bias. In a blind medical trial of a new drug, for example, some test subjects are given the new drug and some are given a placebo, and neither knows which he or she has been given. An experiment is *double-blind* when neither the subjects nor the experimenters know which subjects are in the test and control groups during the experiment. To maintain the integrity of the test, it is important for test subjects to be randomly assigned to the test and control groups. Double-blind experiments are generally considered more scientifically rigorous than blind or nonblind experiments.

The practice of double-blind experimentation can be extended to various areas of cybersecurity. A double-blind penetration test would be one in which the testers are given very little information about the target, perhaps only a name or website, and the target organization is mostly unaware about the test. With this setup, we seek to create a more realistic test by removing the bias that the pen testers had guilty knowledge that real attackers would not have. We also hope to create a realistic situation to test the target organization's security response by not informing them about the test.

Here's another example. You want to compare the detection performance of two malware protection systems. Using a collection of malicious and benign binaries, you randomly select a binary, present it to one of the systems, and observe if the binary is identified as malicious or benign. The experiment is double-blind because neither you nor the malware protection system knows whether the test binary is malicious or not during the test. Of course, you must also have a colleague or program record the actual disposition of each binary in the experiment. After the experiment is over, you can compare how many binaries each malware protection system got right. The benefit of doing a double-blind test in this situation is to remove the real or perceived bias that you, the experimenter, might selectively choose test samples that you know one system might get right or wrong.

The cybersecurity community uses another type of testing called *black box testing*, which may appear to resemble blind testing. In a black box test, the examiner investigates the functionality of the target without knowing how it works. The black box methodology is sometimes used to eliminate examiner bias. In most cases, however, black box testing is used to abstract unnecessary details from testers.

Another time you may hear about double-blind procedures is in the prepublication peer review of scientific papers for conferences and journals. In a double-blind review, the people reviewing the paper are unaware of the authors' identities and the reviewers' identities are likewise concealed from the authors. The primary goal in double-blind review is to avoid biases and conflicts of interest between the reviewers and authors.

Usability Measures: Effectiveness, Efficiency, and Satisfaction

The International Standards Organization (ISO) defines usability as "the effectiveness, efficiency, and satisfaction with which specified users achieve specified goals in particular environments." (ISO 9241-11: Guidance on Usability (1998)). The three defining characteristics are explained as follows:

Effectiveness

> The accuracy and completeness with which specified users can achieve specified goals in particular environments. Example measurements include percentage of goals achieved, functions learned, and errors corrected successfully.

Efficiency

> The resources expended in relation to the accuracy and completeness of goals achieved. Example measurements include the time to complete a task, learning time, and time spent correcting errors.

Satisfaction

> The comfort and acceptability of the work system to its users and other people affected by its use. Example measurements include ratings for satisfaction, ease of learning, and error handling.

A subsequent standard, ISO 20282: Ease of Operation of Every Day Products, makes specific recommendations of design attributes and test methodologies for everyday products. This document makes these five recommendations for easy-to-operate products:

1. Identify the main goal of your product.

2. Identify which user characteristics and which elements of the context of use could affect the ease of operation of your product.

3. Establish the impact of each of these characteristics on the ease of operation of your product.

4. Ensure that the product design takes account of these characteristics.

5. Review the final design to ensure it complies with the characteristics.

One key benefit of these characteristics to science is that they are quantitative in nature. Want to measure the usability of a reverse engineering tool? Give it to a user along with a set of tasks to accomplish using the tool, then measure how many questions she got right, how long it took to complete the questions, and how well she liked the tool. The test methods in ISO 20282 use *effectiveness* as the critical performance measure, defined explicitly as "the percentage of users who achieve the main goal(s) of use of a product accurately and completely."

Of the three usability characteristics, satisfaction is the one that many infosec professionals are unaccustomed to measuring. You have no doubt filled out surveys of this type that measure your satisfaction with a conference or hotel or breakfast cereal. Common practice is to use an ordinal scale with five or fewer points. There is no consensus among experts about whether to use an even or odd point scale, but labeling the points on the scale with descriptive text is preferred to numbers alone. In

---

Figure 11-1, you can see an example scale that you might use with the survey question "How satisfied were you with the reverse engineering tool?"

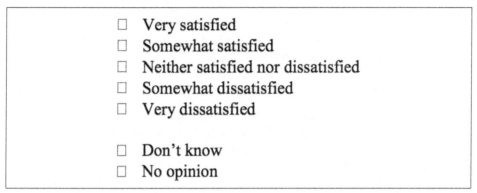

Figure 11-1. A rating scale with five labeled points and two nonscaled choices for a question like "How satisfied were you with the tool?"

Professor Ben Shneiderman at the University of Maryland is an expert on human-computer interaction and information visualization. He has proposed the following Eight Golden Rules of Interface Design in his book *Designing the User Interface*:

1. Strive for consistency

2. Cater to universal usability

3. Offer informative feedback

4. Design dialogs to yield closure

5. Prevent errors

6. Permit easy reversal of actions

7. Support internal locus of control

8. Reduce short-term memory load

These "rules" distill much research into just a few principles and offer a guide to good interaction design. As with most sets of rules, these offer the opportunity to measure and evaluate how well the proposed solution has achieved the desired principle. This list offers another set of usability measures that are complementary to effectiveness, efficiency, and satisfaction. An ideal interface which achieves Shneiderman's principles should score highly in usability.

Let's say you wanted to use Shneiderman's rules as motivation for a test of a new product. Rule #1 is consistency, which is related to predictable and stable language, layout, and design. You could measure consistency in any number of ways. For example, you might compare the training time required to learn Version 1.0 of your software compared to Version 2.0, and find that changes you made to increase consistency directly reduced the amount of training time. On the other hand, you might find that consistency as a primary concern is distracting for users and their work. Or, you might have specialized knowledge about the context in which people will use the product that contradicts the standard rule. If your target users always run EnCase (for forensic analysis) alongside Microsoft Word (for documentation and reporting), you might want to know if consistency between the tools—does Ctrl-S mean *Save* in both?—is more important than the internal consistency of a single tool.

Usability is not necessarily the same as utility and desirability. People use tools with low usability all the time, perhaps because the tools meet a need or achieve an objective. The three usability characteristics can be correlated—high effectiveness may lead to high satisfaction—but may also be independent. Users can be highly effective with a tool but be highly unsatisfied with it.

Finally, let's discuss the difference between beta testing and usability testing. Both beta testing and usability testing are intended to gather user feedback to help developers improve a product. Beta testing typically occurs late in the software development cycle when most design and functionality decisions have already been made. Beta testing provides bug reports and general usage of new features. Usability testing tends to happen before beta testing when there is still time to change fundamental aspects of the solution, and provides insights about whether new features are usable. These two tests are complementary and both should be done when possible. While users often do beta testing in their home or office, and usability testing is sometimes done in a lab, both tests are flexible and amenable to variations in execution.

With these ideas and considerations for *what* data to collect, the next section discusses methods for *how* to collect data.

Methods for Gathering Usability Data

There are many ways to gather usability data. In this section, we'll present some standard methods and other considerations for gathering usability data during two different phases of development: design and validation. Different approaches to usability testing are used during these two phases.

Testing Usability During Design

Usability testing during the design phase is focused on formative assessment, which provides insights about how to improve the design. There are two approaches to usability testing protocols during the tool design phase: moderated and unmoderated.

Moderated data gathering involves the use of a facilitator who observes and/or asks questions as a participant attempts a task, and are often conducted in a controlled setting such as a laboratory. A trained and experienced facilitator can document and solicit very valuable insights about the participant's tool experience during the session. If you have the luxury of time, money, and staff, moderated sessions are a powerful choice.

Unmoderated sessions allow test subjects to provide usability input independently. Remote unmoderated usability testing over the Internet even allows data gathering from the comfort of home. Unmoderated tests are increasingly popular given their convenience and low cost. Remote testing is well suited for web-based interfaces but may be inappropriate for cybersecurity hardware or specialized environments. Remote testing can enable you to more easily draw a large and diverse group of study participants, and several online services can handle participant recruitment, testing, data gathering—even some data analysis.

There are four common approaches for ways of gathering data during usability testing, and one or more may be appropriate for your situation:

- **Concurrent Think Aloud** testing encourages the participant to speak aloud to a (mostly passive) facilitator and explain in a stream of consciousness what he or she is thinking and doing.
- **Retrospective Think Aloud** is a technique where a facilitator asks the participant after the task is complete to orally explain what he or she did. The participant may narrate his or her actions while watching a video replay of the task.
- **Concurrent Probing** involves a facilitator asking probing questions to the participant during the test to solicit details about what or why the participant took a certain action.
- **Retrospective Probing** is a technique for asking the participant probing questions after the session is over. This technique may be done with or without a human facilitator, and may be used along with another method.

In a good usability test, your testers will use your tool to do whatever your real users want to do. Rather than simply asking your testers to "look at" your tool and tell you what they think, come up with a short list of definite tasks—finding a bit of information, collecting and comparing information from different locations, making judgments about the content, etc. Avoid yes/no questions like "Did you think the navigation was clear?" Instead, ask subjects to rate their own responses, as shown in Example 11-1.

Example 11-1. Example usability question

Respond to the following statement: This tool was easy to use.

1. Disagree Strongly
2. Disagree

3. Disagree Somewhat

4. No Opinion

5. Agree Somewhat

6. Agree

7. Agree Strongly

Not only does this allow you to report trends ("Subjects reported an average score of 4.2 for Question 1"), but it allows you to easily quantify changes between tests. Take a look at Table 11-1.

Table 11-1. Improvement between two usability tests as measured by three survey questions

	Test 1	Test 2	Improvement
Q1. The tool is easy to use.	4.2	5.0	+19%
Q2. The tool is too complex.	4.0	3.0	+25%
Q3. The tool could do everything I wanted it to do.	3.0	4.5	+50%

Usability testing allows you to observe what people do and to measure their performance. You are the expert who will use the resulting data to make decisions about whether or not to change the design.

Testing Usability During Validation and Verification

It is important to conduct usability testing when the design is complete, during the validation and verification stage. In this phase, you may want to conduct summative testing. *Summative testing* is used to determine metrics for complete tasks, including time and success rates.

It may be helpful to describe in detail one example of gathering usability data. Assume you just finished creating a new open source network scanning tool. You want to get feedback from users about usability and decide to use retrospective probing. You find some willing participants and give them the tool along with three short questionnaires: pre-test, post-task, and post-test.

Surveys and questionnaires are *prescriptive* methods of data collection because the structure dictates the type and depth of answers that participants provide. The way that questions are asked is very important because the response choices offered strongly affect the responses that participants can provide.

In the pre-test questionnaire, you might want to ask the user's education, age, years of experience, and familiarity with other network scanning tools. The post-task questionnaire includes items related to the task and your desired usability metrics. For example, using a five-point scale (like that in Figure 11-1), ask for agreement with the statement "I was satisfied with the ease of completing this task." In the post-test questionnaire, you can ask structured but free-form questions such as "What are two things about the design that you really liked?" and "What are two things about the design that you didn't like?"

Case Study: An Interface for User-Friendly Encrypted Email

Usable interfaces for email encryption remain an open problem. One of the classic papers in security usability written in 1999 is "Why Johnny Can't Encrypt: A Usability Evaluation of PGP 5.0,"[4] and considers the Pretty Good Privacy (PGP) encryption software that had come out eight years prior in 1991. "We conclude that PGP 5.0 is not usable enough to provide effective security for most computer users," write the authors, "despite its attractive graphical user interface, supporting our hypothesis that user interface design for effective security remains an open problem." In 2015, sixteen years later, usable email encryption and widespread adoption of such solutions remain elusive.

Let's walk through a hypothetical scientific experiment in usability that evaluates secure, encrypted email. Assume that prior work has shown the following assertions about secure email:

- Users will reject secure email if it requires too much effort.
- Users are uninterested and unwilling to obtain or manage cryptographic keys.
- Cryptography is confusing and overwhelming for users, even those who desire security and privacy.

Now assume you work for a university that wants to deploy a Cisco secure email solution called Cisco Registered Envelope Service (CRES), and you want to evaluate its usability as a security product. Companies, universities, and other customers deploy CRES inside their network alongside a traditional email server. To encrypt an email with CRES, the sender simply adds a special keyword like "[secure]" in the email subject line. The email is automatically routed to a secure internal email server where it is encrypted. Email recipients inside the company receive secure email like any non-secure message. External recipients are redirected to a web interface where they regis-

---

4 Alma Whitten and J. D. Tygar. *Why Johnny Can't Encrypt: A Usability Evaluation of PGP 5.0* (Proceedings of the 8th USENIX Security Symposium, 1999).

ter and then view the secure message in a browser. How could you evaluate the usability of this solution?

A New Experiment

For this experiment, you will have a representative group of test subjects perform the task of using CRES. You will gather usability data from the group by collecting measurements that can help you accept or reject this hypothesis:

> University students and faculty will be capable of using CRES to send and receive encrypted email within a reasonable time overhead, and report satisfaction with the experience.

Imagine that the university has 14,000 students and faculty. In order to achieve a 95% confidence level with a 5% confidence interval, a sample size of 374 participants is required. Ideally, you would like a completely random sample of the university population without the added bias of using only freshmen or only computer engineering students. In reality, this goal is often difficult, so let's pretend that you sample from a mandatory course.

In this study plan, we will invite our prospective participants by email to the study website. In a few brief paragraphs, the page describes the purpose of the study (to understand how well users like and perform with encrypted email), the time required (say, 20 minutes), and the benefits to the participant (a chance to influence the ultimate solution). Next we ask a few preliminary questions about computer skills and previous experience with encryption. Then we provide a brief tutorial including step-by-step instructions for using CRES. Then we begin the actual task as follows. Users are instructed to send an encrypted email to the study team at a particular email address. The server records the time when the user logs into the mail server and records when the encrypted message is sent (we could alternatively or additionally ask the user to self-report the amount spent on the task). Your study team later analyzes the study's special mailbox and records the senders who successfully sent them an encrypted message. You also want to test decryption. When the participant is ready, he clicks a web form indicating that he is ready to begin. An automated system sends him an encrypted email and he is instructed to email the decrypted message content to the study's special email address. The server again records the timestamps of each event in this task. Having completed encryption and decryption, you ask the participant how satisfied he was with CRES.

When data collection is complete, you then aggregate and graph the results as shown in Figure 11-2.

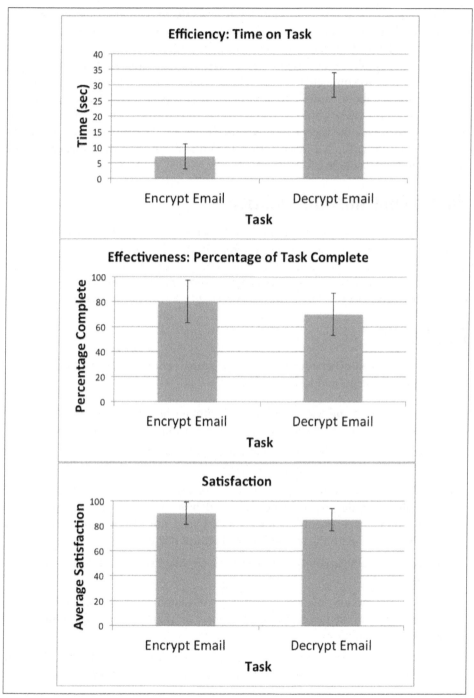

Figure 11-2. Efficiency, effectiveness, and satisfaction with CRES

The data offers insights about how efficiently and effectively users could perform the encryption and decryption task. You might want to dig deeper with statistical analysis into the correlation between effectiveness or efficiency and satisfaction—did users who failed to complete a task report lower satisfaction, or did satisfaction go down the longer it took to complete the task? These results alone are insufficient to make a recommendation about whether to adopt CRES. This data should be compared to a control that in this study would be regular unencrypted email. By performing a well-designed experiment and accepting a hypothesis, you can be confident that the results offer scientifically grounded insights to help you and other decision-makers choose an encrypted email solution.

How to Find More Information

One of the premier venues for human factors research, including usability, is the yearly ACM CHI (Computer-Human Interaction) Conference on Human Factors in Computing Systems. The annual Symposium on Usable Privacy and Security (SOUPS) brings together researchers and practitioners in human-computer interaction, security, and privacy. The Workshop on Usable Security (USEC) is another.

Conclusion

This chapter applied cybersecurity science to human-computer interaction and usability. The key concepts and takeaways are:

- Experimentation and testing in human-computer interaction and usable security are difficult to automate and scale but are highly important to end users.

- Experiments in usability testing include completing specific tasks in a controlled manner and comparing alternative designs.

- Blind experimentation is a procedure where information is concealed from the test subject or the experimenter to avoid human bias in the experiment. In double-blind experiments, neither the subjects nor the experimenters know which subjects are in the test and control groups during the experiment.

- Three measurable usability characteristics are effectiveness, efficiency, and satisfaction.

- Beta testing occurs late in the software development cycle. Usability testing occurs earlier in the design phase while there is still time to change fundamental aspects of the solution.

- Usability experiments can be done during design or validation. Testing during the design phase is focused on providing insights about how to improve the design. Testing during validation is used to determine metrics for complete tasks, including time and success rates.

References

- Lorrie Faith Cranor and Simson Garfinkel. *Security and Usability: Designing Secure Systems that People Can Use* (Boston, MA: O'Reilly Media, 2005)

- Joseph S. Dumas and Janice C. Redish. *A Practical Guide to Usability Testing* (Bristol, UK: Intellect Ltd; Rev Sub edition, 1999)

- Simson Garfinkel and Heather Richter Lipford. *Usable Security: History, Themes, and Challenges* (San Rafael, CA: Morgan & Claypool Publishers, 2014)

- Jonathan Lazar, Jinjuan Feng, and Harry Hochheiser. *Research Methods in Human-Computer Interaction* (Indianapolis, IN: Wiley, 2010)

- Ben Shneiderman and Catherine Plaisant. *Designing the User Interface: Strategies for Effective Human-Computer Interaction: Fifth Edition* (Boston, MA: Addison-Wesley, 2010)

- Symposium on Usable Privacy and Security (SOUPS) (*http://cups.cs.cmu.edu/soups*)

- Stephen A. Thomas. *Data Visualization with JavaScript* (San Francisco, CA: No Starch Press, 2015)

- US Dept. of Health and Human Services (*http://usability.gov*)

## CHAPTER 12

Visualization

Visualization has a reputation in cybersecurity for being glitzy but shallow, more like frosting than cake. However, visualization remains an area of active research and offers an opportunity to apply cybersecurity science. Researcher Danny Quist once posed this as a fundamental visualization question: "How is my tool better than grep?" This question gets at the enormous volume of cybersecurity-related data—especially logs—long dominated by searching and parsing, and grep has been the gold standard cybersecurity tool to beat. This chapter assumes that you are already familiar with the basic concepts and value of visualization and looks at the intersection of science and visualization, how the scientific method can strengthen credibility to visualization by measuring and evaluating how your visualizations are working, and visualization choices to avoid. It also presents a sample case study showing how to experimentally evaluate visualizations in a forensics tool.

Let's start with definitions and terminology. Visualization must be based on nonvisible data, use an image as the primary means of communication, and provide a way to learn something about the data. There are a great deal of pretty pictures created in the name of visualization that fail these criteria, even on the data walls of cybersecurity watch floors and operations centers. Within data visualization there are also many types, including charts, maps, networks, animations, and infographics.

Visualization is a natural match for cybersecurity. The cyber domain has vast amounts of data along with the need to recognize patterns and anomalies. Humans, being part of the cybersecurity process, need to consume and understand data, and vision is the highest-bandwidth human sense. Visualization can support exploration, discovery, decision making, and communication. One famous example of the importance of visualization is Anscombe's quartet, four datasets with nearly identical simple statistical properties that appear very different when graphed (Figure 12-1). As we mentioned in Chapter 2, one of the best ways to start analyzing data is to literally look at it using a graph or chart, even if those visualizations are not the ultimate product.

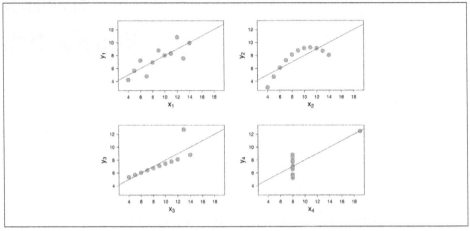

Figure 12-1. Visualization of Anscombe's quartet showing visual differences despite identical simple summary statistics

However, the art and science of visualization for cybersecurity requires knowledge of both cybersecurity and visualization—two skills that few people possess. Deep knowledge and context about cybersecurity data is necessary to create visualizations that are meaningful and useful to users. On the other hand, cybersecurity developers often fail to acknowledge their ignorance in visualization theory, visual efficiency, and human-computer interaction. This knowledge split is best addressed by teams of experts who together can create effective cybersecurity visualizations.

 There is a wide range of open research topics in visualization. Effective human interaction with visualizations remains a challenge for designers, and visualizations of multidimensional data have long been a topic of interest.

An Example Scientific Experiment in Cybersecurity Visualization

For an example of scientific experimentation in cybersecurity visualization, see the paper "Malware Images: Visualization and Automatic Classification" by Nataraj, Karthikeyan, Jacob, and Manjunath (2011).[1] In the abstract that follows, you can see that the hypothesis of this experiment was that visualizations of malware binaries from the same family appear visually similar in layout and texture. This hypothesis was confirmed in experimental tests. You can see the visual similarities in the images from two different malware families in Figure 12-2.[2]

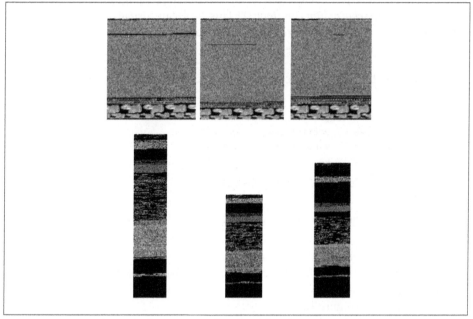

Figure 12-2. Visualization showing two families of malware, the first row belonging to the family Fakerean and the second row belonging to the family Dontovo.A

The authors say that "we went through the thumbnails of [1,713 malware images in 8 malware families] and verified that the images belonging to a family were indeed similar." The experiment could have been further validated by showing the images to unbiased evaluators to measure users' effectiveness, efficiency, and satisfaction.

Abstract from a cybersecurity visualization experiment

We propose a simple yet effective method for visualizing and classifying malware using image processing techniques. Malware binaries are visualized as gray-scale images, with the observation that for many malware families, the images belonging to the same family appear very similar in layout and texture. Motivated by this visual similarity, a

1 L. Nataraj, S. Karthikeyan, G. Jacob, and B. S. Manjunath. 2011. "Malware images: visualization and automatic classification." In *Proceedings of the 8th International Symposium on Visualization for Cyber Security* (VizSec '11). ACM, New York, NY.

2 Image source. (*http://vision.ece.ucsb.edu/~lakshman/nataraj_vizsec_2011_paper.pdf*)

classification method using standard image features is proposed. Neither disassembly nor code execution is required for classification. Preliminary experimental results are quite promising with 98% classification accuracy on a malware database of 9,458 samples with 25 different malware families. Our technique also exhibits interesting resilience to popular obfuscation techniques such as section encryption.

Let's look at one way you could create images of malware using the open source tool, colorize (*http://jessekornblum.com/tools/*). This tool can visualize raw file data and offers one way to visually compare binaries. These images could be used for your own visual similarity study. Here's one approach:

1. Gather the files you want to compare visually. Say you have 10 Windows executables:

   ```
   c:\viz> dir *.exe
   variant1.exe    variant2.exe    variant3.exe    variant4.exe
   variant5.exe    variant6.exe    variant7.exe    variant8.exe
   variant9.exe    variant10.exe
   ```

2. Run colorize on each file to create images:

   ```
   c:\viz> colorize -o -w 512 variant1.exe
   c:\viz> colorize -o -w 512 variant2.exe
   ...
   ```

3. Compare images to each other and see what the visual similarities and differences reveal to you about how these files are related. You may wish to measure how well this visualization helps other experts in a task such as identifying families of malware (Figure 12-3).

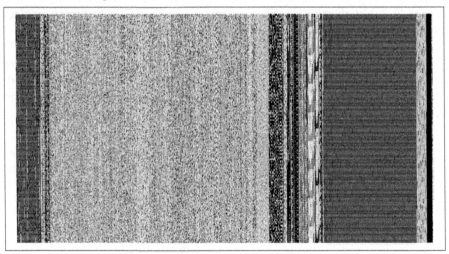

Figure 12-3. Example output of the colorize program showing a visualization of the binary

Graphical Representations of Cybersecurity Data

The goal of visualization should be to aid a human in accomplishing his or her task. Professor Edward Tufte, statistician and prominent author on data visualization, wrote that "indeed graphics can be more precise and revealing than conventional statistical computations."[3]

Visualization to Aid Cyber Challenges

A 2014 study identified the following seven challenges faced by cyber defenders. You can imagine that each might be improved with the help of visualization. Scientific inquiry could help evaluate *how well* a visualization has helped improve the challenge.

- Lots of data
- Lots of data sources
- Data sources not linked
- Data quality
- Cadence of the network
- Progression of threat escalation
- Balancing risk and reward

Security and network administrators faced with these challenges may be familiar with the visualization capabilities of their security tools today. For example, Splunk (*http://www.splunk.com*) is a well-known commercial package for analyzing data such as logs, and includes native visualization capabilities. Kibana (*https://www.elastic.co/products/kibana*) is an open source data visualization platform and is often used in conjunction with two other log processing and searching tools, Logstash and Elasticsearch. As you can see in Figure 12-4 and Figure 12-5, these platforms offer traditional types of graphics including bar graphs, pie graphs, histograms, and world maps.

---

3 Edward Tufte. *The Visual Display of Quantitative Information.* (Graphics Press, 1983).

Figure 12-4. An example of cybersecurity visualizations from Splunk using data from the Cisco Identity Services Engine (http://bit.ly/1NPWLn8)

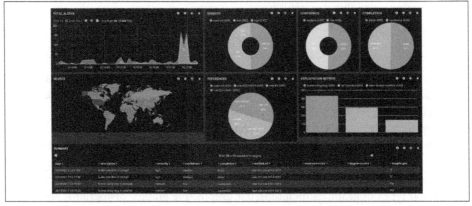

Figure 12-5. An example of open source visualization using Hakabana (http://www.haka-security.org/hakabana.html), a Kibana dashboard for Haka security alerts

Unfortunately, visualizations are often used inappropriately, leading intentionally or unintentionally to ambiguity or cognitive bias of the viewer. Let's look at the challenges associated with one kind of visualization: the pie chart. You might consider pie charts one of many equal choices for displaying data, but there are actually appropriate and inappropriate uses for pie charts. The basic premise of a pie chart is that the pie represents a meaningful whole. Don't use a pie chart if the sum of the slices doesn't add up to 100%. Data represented in the pie chart must also be unique to one slice—they cannot be counted in more than one slice. Another unfortunate problem with pie charts is that human viewers are not very good about judging the angle (and therefore relative size) of a slice. Research suggests that people have low confidence and low accuracy in reading pie charts, and that people's perception of the slices can be manipulated simply by rotating the pie. As a result, it is better to use pie charts to illustrate comparisons of the slices to the whole, not to compare slices to each other. Therefore, consider the pie chart only when there are few slices (fewer than five to seven), when the parts are mutually exclusive, when the slices make up a meaningful whole, and when you want to show part-whole relationships. Examples of pie charts can be seen in Appendix A.

For more examples of good and bad illustrations of quantative information, visit Perceptual Edge (*http://www.perceptualedge.com/ examples.php*).

Ben Shneiderman, a visualization expert, developed his own visual information-seeking mantra: overview first, zoom and filter, then details-on-demand.[4] While not a set of evaluation criteria per se, the mantra summarizes many visual design guidelines and provides a framework for designing cybersecurity visualizations. These principles have been validated with scientific studies showing that they measurably improve human use of visualizations.

Science can help with cybersecurity visualization in determining two important criteria: how to visualize and how to evaluate visualizations. Choices about how to visualize data should be informed by psychological, behavioral, and cultural science. Consider something as routine as color choice. Say you want to display computer infections on a colored map. Imagine the Norse Attack Map (*http://map.norse corp.com*) in Figure 12-6 colored all red or all green.

---

4 Ben Shneiderman. "The Eyes Have It: A Task by Data Type Taxonomy for Information Visualizations." In *Proceedings of the IEEE Symposium on Visual Languages* (IEEE Computer Society Press, 1996).

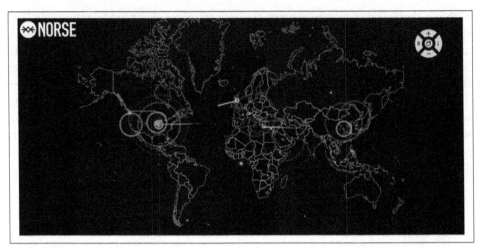

Figure 12-6. Norse attack map

Here are some questions to ask when choosing one color over another:

- Will people with red–green color blindness have difficulty interpreting the graphic?
- Will the graphic be seen and interpreted differently by people in China, where red is associated with good fortune, and the United States, where red can symbolize danger?
- Is red an appropriate color for the environments where the graphic is likely to appear, such as a dimly lit security watch floor?
- Will the color produce an illegible image if printed in black and white?

All of these learned or cultural assumptions can affect the ultimate usefulness of the visualization, and each can be measured and evaluated to maximize the choices.

Scientifically informed deliberate choices about visualizations can also be tested, and the next section will look more in depth at how to use experimentation to evaluate visualizations.

Experimental Evaluation of Security Visualization

Chapter 11 discussed three usability measures: effectiveness, efficiency, and satisfaction. A key challenge for visualization is evaluating if and how a visualization meets these criteria. You may wish to test hypotheses such as *this new tool effectively conveys information to a novice user*, or *users are satisfied when using my tool to solve a problem*.

There is no universal approach and no single way to evaluate all security visualizations. In fact, there is no consensus in the visualization community about what *constitutes* an evaluation. Different metrics and assessment techniques should be applied depending on the purpose and scope of the evaluation. In addition to the three usability measures mentioned above, some evaluations will consider other factors such as the effect on collaboration, cognitive workload, and component interoperability.

User studies are an important method for evaluating cybersecurity visualizations. These studies can help you pinpoint why a particular visualization is effective or not with the target user population. Finding users to test your hypotheses can be challenging, and different users are appropriate in different situations (e.g., expertise, age, nationality). It is important to understand your test subjects to recognize and account for biases that they may bring to the experiment.

When you look at how researchers conduct experimental evaluations of visualizations, there are four general types of evaluation:

- **Controlled experiments comparing design elements**. This category compares different types or implementations of a specific widget (e.g., a world map) or compares how well nonvisual data maps to a graphical representation. This is a *controlled experiment* because it changes exactly one variable while keeping other variables constant.

- **Usability evaluation**. This area is composed of studies that allow users to interact with a tool and provide feedback to the developers and designers about effectiveness, efficiency, and satisfaction, or allows the experimenter to measure and evaluate those criteria

- **Controlled experiments comparing two or more tools**. This category compares the differences in effectiveness, efficiency, and satisfaction between different tools with the same goal. Generally, these studies compare a new tool with similar existing tools.

- **Real-world case studies**. This area is composed of research and reports describing how real users in natural environments perform their real tasks. These studies can be very specific to the users or the environment and have low external validity (generalizability to other situations).

One or more of these evaluation types may be appropriate for your situation. Within each type are a variety of evaluation techniques, some of which are experimental. Surveys, for example, allow you to gather quantitative and qualitative data, but a survey is not an experimental evaluation. On the other hand, if you used interface instrumentation to collect usage and user interaction information, this technique could be used to collect data in a controlled experiment. Simulations are another common evaluation technique because they offer control over the experiment while incorporating realistic scenarios and conditions. One of the more advanced techniques is psychophysiological measurements, such as eye tracking, heart rate, and brain measurements taken during a user's interaction with a visualization.

Let's look at a slightly modified version of a usability evaluation. In Figure 12-7, the researcher wants to see if test subjects can correctly answer questions using the new visualization by asking a task-based question.

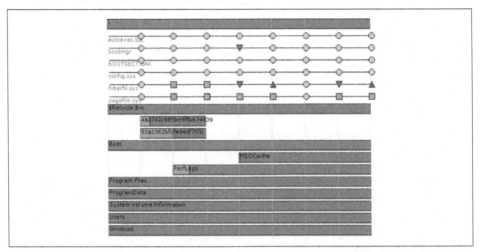

Figure 12-7. User evaluation question: How many subdirectories exist within the root ("\") directory?

In a subsequent part of the study, the developer may give the subject the answer in order to solicit feedback about why the subject got the answer wrong, and the user's satisfaction with the visualization (see Figure 12-8).

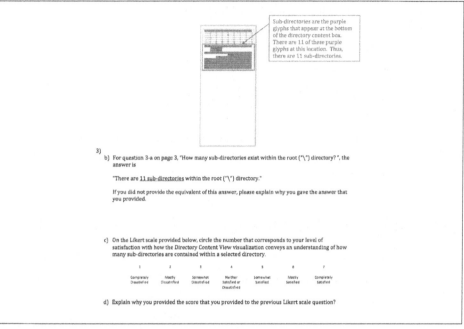

Figure 12-8. User evaluation, continued

Execution of a User Study

Here are some generic steps to follow when executing a user study. Adjust these steps depending on the task and the participants, but consider some version of these steps even for informal evaluations with people you know. It is recommended that you create a script to read to participants, ensuring that you cover everything in the same way with each participant. Remember, reproducibility is a principle of the scientific method.

1. Greet and welcome the participant and introduce yourself.

2. Thank the participant for his or her participation.

3. Explain the broad evaluation goals and why you need the participant's help.

4. Walk through the entire study process with the participant.

5. Make sure that the participant knows what is expected of him or her during the experiment, and seek consent if necessary.

6. Describe the study to the participant in an appropriate amount of detail.

7. Inform the participant that you will be collecting metrics (e.g., accuracy) and explicitly state important items that will not be measured (e.g., time).

8. Answer any questions that the participant may have about the study or the process.

9. Ask the participant to complete the task.

10. Collect any post-task data as desired, such as a survey or questionnaire.

11. Thank the participant for completing the study.

As you can tell, there are a wide variety of approaches to evaluation, each with its own tradeoffs. Experimental evaluation will help you evaluate how the visualization is meeting your intended goals, improve the product, and compare one visualization to another.

Case Study: Is My Visualization Helping Users Work More Effectively?

In this section, we walk through a hypothetical scientific experiment in security visualization. In this experiment, we will perform an experimental evaluation of a fictitious tool called EvidenceViz, which visualizes a digital forensic disk image in an attempt to more quickly draw a human's attention to potential evidence.

There are numerous options for measuring a user's performance. One is to measure user accuracy at performing a certain task. Another is to measure the time required to perform the task. A third is to measure emotional responses, such as the confidence the user has in her answer (indicating effectiveness). Yet another is qualitative feedback as in a questionnaire. Tool developers and researchers sometimes have to use their judgment about which evaluation is the most useful or compelling for other people who will use or critique the tool. No specific measurement is necessarily expected or required for a given solution, though there are trends in academic evaluations toward usability testing and simulation, and very few longitudinal studies—repeated observations of the same user(s) over time—and interface instrumentations.

The goal of this testing is to help the efficacy of the new visualization technique by narrowly evaluating one aspect: time required to perform a task. Given our desire to measure the effectiveness of the visualization at helping a forensic analyst identify evidence of cyber crime based on the time spent on the task, here is a hypothesis:

> Forensic analysts will find specific evidence of cyber crime faster using EvidenceViz than with EnCase.

EnCase and FTK are two of the most popular forensic tools, and the independent variables in the experiment are the visualization techniques, yours and theirs. The null hypothesis is that your visualization is not more effective than the currently used techniques. The scientific method says that we must keep all other variables in the experiment constant. In particular, we want to create an experiment where test subjects will perform the same task, described next, but one randomly assigned group will use EvidenceViz and another group will use EnCase or FTK.

The task performed by forensic analyst test subjects should reflect realistic work. The discovery and identification of digital images is a very common forensic task because photographs are part of many crimes. For the purposes of this experiment, we want a hard drive image that is realistic but controlled. For many reasons, including legal and ethical, you should not use a forensic image from a real-life crime. There are differing opinions about the degree of realism required. You may benefit from using a preexisting scenario-based image (*http://digitalcorpora.org*), or may wish to create a new image of your own. If you create a new image, consider ways to make it look realistic, such as by browsing Internet websites and creating documents. Then, plant the data (e.g., images of cats) that you intend the visualization tools to help the test subjects find.

 There are numerous considerations when creating realistic data for experimentation. For more on one experience creating forensic evidence in a realistic scenario, see "Creating Realistic Corpora for Forensic and Security Education" by Woods et al. (2011).

In this particular user study, we must make a trade-off. Either the same study participants will see the same forensic image in multiple visualization tools, or individual participants will see the forensic image in only one tool. Using the same people eliminates individual differences but biases the experiment because the task requires the participant to find something, and he or she will likely know the answer after the first test. On the other hand, when only one set of participants sees a particular technique, you cannot isolate effects from individual differences and it requires more participants. There is no general consensus about how many participants are needed in a usability study. There have been empirical results endorsing the specific number of participants as 4 ± 1, 10 ± 2, and various other formulas. You also want to consider whether to specify or randomize other attributes of the participants, including experience. You should consider giving users at least a basic primer on new or unfamiliar tools to rule out the bias in completion time from familiarity with one tool over another.

With these considerations in mind, assume you are able to find 20 volunteers who all have equivalent experience as forensic analysts, 10 each for EvidenceViz and EnCase. You bring in each participant, explain the experiment, allow him or her to complete the task with one of the visualization tools, and time how long it takes to complete the task. The specific task isn't important, and could be finding a set of images or constructing an event timeline. When you calculate the results, you could find that on average it took 10.49 minutes to complete the task with EnCase and 7.10 minutes with EvidenceViz. Using this evidence, you can accept the hypothesis with proof that for this group of people in this situation, people found evidence faster with Evidence-Viz than EnCase.

 Be careful about the claims you make from this study. It did not prove that EvidenceViz is universally "better" than EnCase. The results must be viewed from the narrow lens of the specific task, the specific test subjects, the specific software versions, and other characteristics of the experiment.

How to Find More Information

Research in visualization is presented at various conferences, but especially at the IEEE Visualization Conference (VIS), the Workshop on Visualization for Cyber Security (VizSec), and the IEEE Visual Analytics Science and Technology (VAST) Conference. The Visual Analytics Benchmark Repository (*http://hcil2.cs.umd.edu/newvarepository/*) is a useful collection of ground truth datasets for use in visualization research.

Conclusion

This chapter looked at the intersection of science and visualization. The key concepts and takeaways are:

- Deep knowledge and context about cybersecurity data is necessary to create visualizations that are meaningful and useful to users.

- In one example, experimental tests showed that visualizations of malware binaries from the same family appear visually similar in layout and texture.

- Cybersecurity science can be used to evaluate whether or not a visualization aids a human in accomplishing his or her task. When used inappropriately, visualizations may intentionally or unintentionally lead to ambiguity or cognitive bias of the viewer.

- There are four general types of visualization evaluations: controlled experiments comparing design elements, usability evaluation, controlled experiments comparing two or more tools, and real-world case studies.

References

- Greg Conti. *Security Data Visualization: Graphical Techniques for Network Analysis* (San Francisco, CA: No Starch Press, 2007)

- Noah Iliinsky and Julie Steele. *Designing Data Visualizations* (Boston, MA: O'Reilly Media, 2011)

- InfoViz Wiki (*http://www.infovis-wiki.net*)

- Raffael Marty. *Applied Security Visualization* (Boston, MA: Addison-Wesley Professional, 2008)

- Edward R. Tufte. *The Visual Display of Quantitative Information* (Cheshire, CT: Graphics Press, 2001)

Understanding Bad Science, Scientific Claims, and Marketing Hype

There is a pop song from the 1980s called "She Blinded Me with Science" that plays on the notion of deliberately hiding truth behind real or made-up science. In this book, I talked about the amazing benefits of science to everyday cybersecurity. Unfortunately, not every scientific claim that you see in the news or from vendors is as reputable as it should be. This appendix will look briefly at the ways in which people are misled, manipulated, or deceived by real or bogus science, scientific claims, and marketing trickery.

Scientific skepticism is a healthy practice of questioning scientific results and claims. In particular, it often means discerning whether the conclusions are the result of the scientific method and are supported by empirical research. This can be very challenging even in the best circumstances, and especially difficult when advertisers and marketers might be appealing to your emotions instead of rationality.

Vendors and marketers sometimes appeal to people's scientific gullibility. As discussed early in the book, people respect and trust science. Unfortunately, people can also be over trusting and thus deceived by scientific claims if they don't possess the experience, healthy suspicion, and rational thinking. One academic study actually found that people were swayed by advertisements with graphs and formulas just because they *seemed* scientific:[1]

> The appearance of being scientific can increase persuasiveness. Even trivial cues can create such an appearance of a scientific basis. In our studies, including simple elements, such as graphs (Studies 1–2) or a chemical formula (Study 3), increased belief

---

1 Aner Tal and Brian Wansink. "Blinded with science: Trivial graphs and formulas increase ad persuasiveness and belief in product efficacy." *Public Understanding of Science* (2014).

in a medication's efficacy. This appears to be due to the association of such elements with science, rather than increased comprehensibility, use of visuals, or recall. Belief in science moderates the persuasive effect of graphs, such that people who have a greater belief in science are more affected by the presence of graphs (Study 2). Overall, the studies contribute to past research by demonstrating that even trivial elements can increase public persuasion despite their not truly indicating scientific expertise or objective support.

Graphics can help explain and clarify data, but don't be swayed by visualizations alone. Cybersecurity "attack maps," for example, might not show the quality data you'd expect. Instead, they may be populated by "beautifully animated yet unfiltered, unverified, non-prioritized event data that while visually compelling is worthless from a security perspective," says one CEO of an Internet security company.[2]

 BAHFest, the Festival of Bad Ad-Hoc Hypotheses, which started in 2013 at MIT, is a satirical conference organized by evolutionary biologists for their own entertainment. Speakers present serious-sounding talks about bogus, made-up (but funny) scientific claims.

In the following sections, we will look at specific ways of communicating scientific results that you should be aware of as you evaluate cybersecurity products and services.

Dangers of Manipulative Graphics and Visualizations

Chapter 12 explored ways to create and scientifically evaluate visualizations. It also looked at a few cautionary notes, such as how color can carry cultural or symbolic significance. Graphics and visualizations are an important mechanism for communicating scientific results and complex data. Visual communication can supplement and sometimes simplify complex and dense text. Humans may even process visual information faster than text. But viewers beware, visualizations aren't always what they seem.

Bad visualization choices can do more harm than good. Viewers are manipulated by bad visualizations because of mental shortcomings and perception, not necessarily because the visualization is incorrect. Look at Figure A-1. It is nearly impossible to distinguish the distinctions in size between the pie slices. The visualization here is probably unhelpful to most viewers.

---

2 Paul Vixie, *Internet Security Marketing: Buyer Beware.* (*http://www.circleid.com/posts/20150420_inter net_security_marketing_buyer_beware/*)

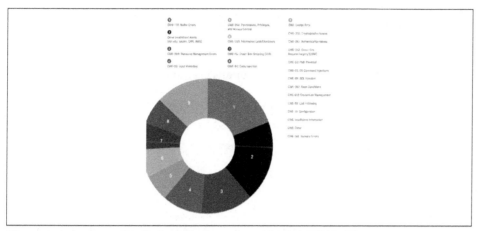

Figure A-1. An example of a bad pie chart (http://bit.ly/1Nl9NpG)

Figure A-2 illustrates other visualization choices. The pie charts on the left offer little visual aid because it is difficult to see any difference between them, even though they are displayed in such a way that the viewer is expected to compare them. The bar charts are easier to compare, though they lack axis labels, a key feature.

Figure A-2. An example of visually challenging visualizations (http://symc.ly/1OoIWyY)

Some graphics are manipulative because of the data they omit. Look at Figure A-3. First, the image is supposed to support the claim that "Ad-Aware significantly outperforms our free peers." That short statement uses two words, "significantly" and "peers," that are not defined and which potentially affect the interpretation of the claim. The graphic shows two peers, for example. The viewer could assume (incorrectly) that there are no others missing from the comparison. The data in the visualization also raises questions. If 393 malware samples were tested, how were those files chosen? Were they randomly selected or hand-picked for easy detection by this product? What was the false positive rate? We are told how many files each product "missed," presumably indicating false negatives, but the antivirus products could have also incorrectly identified many benign files as malicious. As you evaluate cybersecurity products and as you report data about your own products, be aware of what the conclusions and graphics are and aren't telling you.

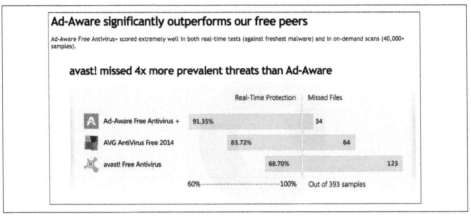

Figure A-3. Ad-Aware by Lavasoft (http://bit.ly/1Nl9ATl) in-house performance results

Recognizing and Understanding Scientific Claims

In 2004, *Popular Science* published an article documenting one writer's encounters with science claims in a typical day. He counted 106, starting with his breakfast cereal box. You encounter a lot of scientific claims because advertising is everywhere and advertisers are in the business of making claims. Recognizing the positive spin that advertisers naturally seek is important when you have to make a decision about whether to use, buy, or believe that product. Having read this book, you are already ahead of the curve. According to the National Science Board's 2002 study "Science and Engineering Indicators," only one-third of Americans can "adequately explain what it means to study something scientifically."

Scientific claims may be easy to recognize. Here are some examples:

- Tests show that Product A can detect 97% of sophisticated malware.
- Our forensic imaging software is twice as fast as competing products.
- Company B's fingerprint reader is 99.9% accurate.
- Alice Corp. is better at detecting insider threats than Bob Corp.
- Nine out of ten websites we scanned on the Internet are vulnerable to the XYZ attack.

Scientific claims tend to be obvious because they are being used to promote or sell a product or service.

One of the marketing phrases that immediately raises flags for me is when something is "scientifically proven." This phrase is misguided because scientific conclusions are never absolutely certain. All empirical evidence has some margin of error, however small. Furthermore, scientific models don't have to be 100% correct to be valid. It is

---

dangerous to believe that the scientific truth we believe now cannot be updated with new evidence or new interpretations of the evidence.

There is a well-known book by Darrell Huff titled *How to Lie with Statistics* (1954) that documents ways in which numbers and statistics are sometimes presented to support a lie. As a trivial example, consider the ambiguous meaning of the word "average." The description of a scientific result should use a precise mathematical word: mean, median, or mode. While all three describe the data truthfully, choosing one and calling it the "average" may be misleading. For example, someone might say "the average company lost $10 million due to cybersecurity compromises last year." What does that mean? The answer depends greatly on the number of companies sampled and the distribution of the values. In Table A-1, the "average loss" could be reported as $750,000 (median), $1 million (mode), or $20 million (mean).

Table A-1. Financial losses for five fictitious victims in 2014 (median=$750,000; mode=$1M; mean=$20M)

Company	Financial Loss From Cyber Attacks in 2014
Victim #1	$0
Victim #2	$500,000
Victim #3	$500,000
Victim #4	$1,000,000
Victim #5	$1,000,000
Victim #6	$100,000,000

One company issues an often-quoted report on the global cost of data breaches. The report includes this poignant disclaimer of a reason to be skeptical of the results: "Our study draws upon a representative, non-statistical sample of U.S.-based entities experiencing a breach involving the loss or theft of customer or consumer records during the past 12 months. Statistical inferences, margins of error and confidence intervals cannot be applied to these data given that *our sampling methods are not scientific* [emphasis added]." There may be other reasons to trust this report, but prudent readers should make a calculated and cautious choice.

You should be especially skeptical about vendor-sponsored reports, since the vendor has a financial incentive to make its product look good. There may be vendors that you trust to report unbiased facts even if those facts don't support the vendor. It is still wise to be cautious and ask yourself what, if anything, the vendor has to gain by the data. FireEye, a respected cybersecurity company, had this headline on its website: "FireEye NX Series Achieves 99% Detection Rate."[3] Below the headline it said "Third-

---

3 FireEye, *How Cyber Attacks Compromise Your Network* (*http://bit.ly/1Nl9ICe*), retrieved June 1, 2015.

party vendor, Delta Testing, tested a number of vendors using real-world advanced malware. Read the full report to find out the results." If you clicked on the link and read the report cover-to-cover, you could find this disclaimer on the last page: "Fire-Eye sponsored the execution of this test and chose the vendors selected."[4]

Surveys are a fertile ground for abuse. Among the red flags you should watch for are surveys that fail to disclose the survey methodology, sample size, and margin of error. A survey found that a surprising 89% of infosec professionals think that DDoS attacks are the biggest threat to their company. Here is how selection bias might skew that statistic by making it larger than reality. You start by buying an email list from a reputable marketing firm. Your email to the list includes a link to the survey, with a note that respondents must be infosec professionals. You also promise that by completing the survey, the respondent will be entered for a chance to win a $50 gift card. When your survey is over, you may very well have gotten 89% of respondents who say that DDoS attacks are the top threat. However, there is a strong selection bias because the respondents were those who clicked on the email and self-selected as infosec professionals.

In his book and website *Spurious Correlations*, Tyler Vigen explores various scenarios in which data can be combined in surprising and often humorous ways. He says of himself, "...I do have a love for science and discovery and that's all anyone should need." The word "spurious" means fake, bogus, or fraudulent, and the charts on Vigen's site intentionally illustrate such correlations. Consider, for example, Figure A-4, which charts actual US spending on science, space, and technology (as reported by the Office of Management and Budget) with suicides by hanging, strangulation, and suffocation (as reported by the Centers for Disease Control and Prevention). Because the graphs have a similar shape, it might appear that these unrelated statistics are correlated when in fact they are totally independent.

---

4 Delta Testing, *A New Approach to Assessing Advanced Threat Solutions* (*http://bit.ly/1Nl9GKH*), retrieved June 1, 2015.

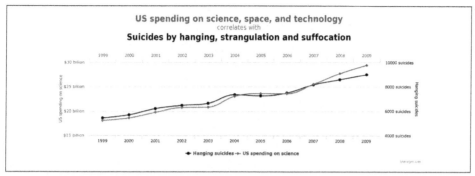

*Figure A-4. A spurious correlation of two unrelated statistics (http://www.tylervi
gen.com/spurious-correlations)*

Vendor Marketing

"Attackers have significantly decreased the cost of obtaining sensitive track data."
How often do you see phrases like this one, which appeared in a vendor security
report? What does *significantly* mean here? Marketing strategist David Meerman
Scott calls this kind of language "gobbledygook," including such phrases as "market
leading," "groundbreaking," and "next generation."

Look at the press release in Figure A-5. This article describes the results of an evaluation from NSS Labs, an independent security research company. One NSS slogan is
"At NSS, we make security a science." So far, so good. Fortinet describes the product
that was tested as an "advanced persistent threats breach detection system" but takes
liberty in saying that the product "achieves high rankings for APT threat detection"
because NSS never claims that it tests advanced threats, only "real-world" traffic (Fortinet also does not define APT). It is good to see a false positive rate reported, but no
false negative rate is given. We aren't told how many, if any, nonmalicious events were
incorrectly identified as malicious.

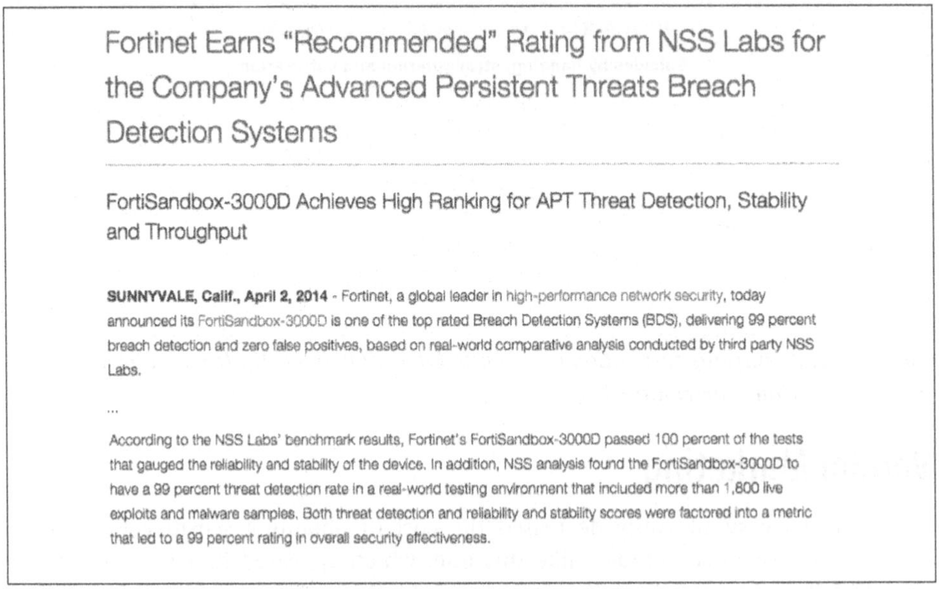

Fortinet Earns "Recommended" Rating from NSS Labs for the Company's Advanced Persistent Threats Breach Detection Systems

FortiSandbox-3000D Achieves High Ranking for APT Threat Detection, Stability and Throughput

SUNNYVALE, Calif., April 2, 2014 - Fortinet, a global leader in high-performance network security, today announced its FortiSandbox-3000D is one of the top rated Breach Detection Systems (BDS), delivering 99 percent breach detection and zero false positives, based on real-world comparative analysis conducted by third party NSS Labs.

...

According to the NSS Labs' benchmark results, Fortinet's FortiSandbox-3000D passed 100 percent of the tests that gauged the reliability and stability of the device. In addition, NSS analysis found the FortiSandbox-3000D to have a 99 percent threat detection rate in a real-world testing environment that included more than 1,800 live exploits and malware samples. Both threat detection and reliability and stability scores were factored into a metric that led to a 99 percent rating in overall security effectiveness.

Figure A-5. A Fortinet press release (http://bit.ly/1OoJvJi)

Let's assume that salespeople are doing their best to communicate with you, that their use of ambiguous terms or lack of convincing evidence is innocent and isn't intended to deceive you. The questions in the next section may help you dig deeper and get answers to help you evaluate the quality and trustworthiness of their products or research results. And in the unfortunate case where the salesperson *is* trying to hide the shortcomings of the product or research, these questions may also help reveal that situation.

Clarifying Questions for Salespeople, Researchers, and Developers

Your experience and expertise are valuable when learning and evaluating new technology. The first time you read about a new cybersecurity development or see a new product, chances are that your intuition will give you a sense for the value and utility of that result for you. As we've seen in this appendix, vendors, marketers, even researchers are trying to convince you of something. It can be helpful for you to have some clarifying questions ready which probe deeper through the sales pitch. Whether you're chatting with colleagues, reading an academic paper, or talking with an exhibitor at a conference, these questions might help you decide for yourself whether the product or experimental results are valid.

- Who did the work? Are there any conflicts of interest?

- Who paid for the work and why was it done?
- Did the experimentation or research follow the scientific method? Is it repeatable?
- How were the experimental or evaluation dataset or test subjects chosen?
- How large was the sample size? Was it truly representative?
- What is the precision associated with the results, and does it support the implied degree of accuracy?
- What are the factually supported conclusions, and what are the speculations?
- What is the sampling error?
- What was the developer or researcher looking for when the result was found? Was he or she biased by expectations?
- What other studies have been done on this topic? Do they say the same thing? If they are different, why are they different?
- Do the graphics and visualizations help convey meaningful information without manipulating the viewer?
- Are adverbs like "significantly" and "substantially" describing the product or research sufficiently supported by evidence?
- The product seems to be supported primarily by anecdotes and testimonials. What is the supporting evidence?
- How did you arrive at causation for the correlated data/event?
- Who are the authors of the study or literature? Are they credible experts in their field?
- Do the results hinge on rare or extreme data that could be attributed to anomalies or non-normal conditions?
- What is the confidence interval of the result?

In the 1990s, numerous journals in medicine, psychology, and ecology underwent an editorial shift to requiring confidence intervals and discouraging sole reliance on statistical hypothesis testing (such as p values) because authors were routinely misusing and misinterpreting significance tests.[5]

5 F. Fidler, G. Cumming, M. Burgman, N. J. Thomason. Statistical reform in medicine, psychology and ecology, *The Journal of Socio-Economics* 33, 615–630 (2004).

- Are the conclusions based on predictions extrapolated from different data than the actual data?
- Are the results based on rare occurrences? What is the likelihood of the condition occurring?
- Has the result been confirmed or replicated by multiple, independent sources?
- Was there *no effect*, no effect *detected*, or *a nonsignificant effect*?
- Even if the results are statistically significant, is the effect size so small that the result is unimportant?

For more red flags of bad science, see the *Science or Not* blog (*http://scienceornot.net/science-red-flags/*).

References

- Hamid Ghanadan. *Persuading Scientists: Marketing to the World's Most Skeptical Audience* (Nashville, TN: RockBench Publishing Corp, 2012)
- Noah J. Goldstein, Steve J. Martin, and Robert B. Cialdini. *Yes!: 50 Scientifically Proven Ways to Be Persuasive* (New York, NY: Free Press, 2009)
- Darrell Huff. *How to Lie with Statistics* (New York, NY: W. W. Norton & Company, 1954)
- Alex Reinhart. *Statistics Done Wrong: The Woefully Complete Guide,* (San Francisco, CA: No Starch Press, 2015)
- David Meerman Scott. *The New Rules of Marketing & PR,* Fourth Edition (Indianapolis, IN: Wiley, 2013)
- Michael Shermer. *Why People Believe Weird Things: Pseudoscience, Superstition, and Other Confusions of Our Time,* (New York, NY: Holt Paperbacks, 2002)

Index

DGAs (domain generation algorithms), 69
digital forensics
    about, 89
    comparison of tool performance, 94-96
    reproducibility and repeatability, 93
    scientific experiments in, 89-90
    scientific validity and, 90-93
Digital Forensics Research Workshop
    (DFRWS), 96
DigitalCorpora.org website, 94
DIMVA Conference, 64
distributed denial-of-service (DDoS), 85
DLP (data loss prevention) technology, 120-121
DNA profiling, 107
domain generation algorithms (DGAs), 69
double-blind experiments, 128
DSN (Dependable Systems and Networks)
    Conference, 122
dynamic analysis, 42, 100

E

EAL (evaluation assurance level), 41
ecological validity, 32
effectiveness (usability), 130, 152-154
efficiency (usability), 130
ElGamal crypto algorithm, 80
email encryption, 135-138
emergent properties, 85
empirical method, 7
EnCase software, 92, 152-154
encryption
    email, 135-138
    evaluating effectiveness of, 79-80
    experiment with, 86-87
Enron Corpus public dataset, 34
evaluation assurance level (EAL), 41
experimentation (see cybersecurity experimen-
    tation; scientific experiments)
!exploitable crash analyzer, 48
exploratory data analysis, 23
external validity, 20

F

Fahrenheit-Celsius temperature conversion,
    116
fair tests, 19-20
false negatives, 55-58
false positives, 55-58, 92
falsifiability (scientific method), 6, 8

Farid, Hany, 91
file-path translator, 90
FireEye provider, 103, 161
FlowMonitor module (ns-3), 101
forensics, digital (see digital forensics)
formal methods, 44
Frye standard, 91
FTK tool, 152
fuzzing method, 42, 43-44

G

Galileo utility, 49
Gambit software, 106
game theory
    about, 5, 103
    for malware analysis, 103-106
    for security resource allocation, 104
GameSec Conference, 108
Gams software, 106
Gauss, Carl Friedrich, 77
Gershengorn, Dana, 91
get-aduser cmdlet, 115
GitHub repository, 25
GNU Privacy Guard (GPG), 80
Google
    PageRank algorithm, 7
    sharing results in public domain, 25
    speech recognition, 70
    translation tool, 90
Gordin, Michael, 10
GPG (GNU Privacy Guard), 80
graphical representations of data, 145-148,
    158-159
grep tool, 141
GUARDS algorithm, 104
guessing, untested, 3

H

HackerOne, 103
HDFS (Hadoop Distributed File System), 67, 94
Heartbleed bug, 48
hindsight bias, 12
Homeland Security, Department of, 41, 103
Honeynet Project, 102
honeypots, 104
hping3 tool, 57
HSR (human subjects research), 35
Huff, Darrell, 161
human factors

A Mathematical Theory of Cryptography
(Shannon), 80
MATLAB software, 116
Maxion, Roy, 65
McAfee ePolicy Orchestrator, 114
mean (analytical method), 22
measurements (metrics) (see metrics (measurements))
Mechanical Turk (Amazon), 38
median (analytical method), 22
metrics (measurements)
    CVSS scores, 48
    false negative rate, 57
    false positive rate, 57
    for encryption, 79
    performance benchmarks, 59
    role of, 12
    Snort detection performance, 60-63
    usability, 129-132
Microsoft Research, 3, 44
mode (analytical method), 22
modeling
    adversarial models, 46-47, 81
    in test environments, 32-33
Morris worm, 53
moving target defense, 5, 105, 118
mutually assured destruction, 104
Mytob malware family, 106

N

Nagios monitoring program, 73-75
Nash equilibrium, 104
Nash, John Forbes, Jr., 104
National Science Board, 160
National Science Foundation, 25
National Security Agency
    block ciphers and, 83
    lablets and, 10
    open datasets, 34
National Vulnerability Database, 49
NDSS (symposium), 122
Netflix and Chaos Monkey, 118
network monitoring
    data mining for, 70-73
    human factor in, 68-70
    machine learning for, 70-73
neural networks, 70-73
Nielsen, Jakob, 126
no free lunch theorems, 73

Norse attack map, 147
Novum Organum (Bacon), 7
ns-3 simulator, 101
NSS Labs, 163
NStreamAware system, 66
null hypothesis, 16-17, 62, 152
NVisAware application, 66

O

objectivity (scientific method), 8
observer effect, 31
open datasets, 34, 72
overconfidence bias, 12

P

p-value, 23
PageRank algorithm, 7
password cracking, 36
penetration testing, 42
perfect secrecy notion, 80
performance
    of cryptographic algorithms, 78-80
    of forensic tools, 94-96
    of intrusion detection, 58-63
Petroski, Henry, 9
PGP (Pretty Good Privacy), 135
pie charts, 146, 159
Pinoccio Scouts, 86
PKI (public key infrastructure), 112
plaintext attacks, 79
PlanetLab testbed, 37
plot command (R), 116
PointToPointHelper class, 101
Popper, Karl, 6
Practical Malware Analysis (Sikorski), 99
PREDICT datasets, 34
predictability (scientific method), 8
Pretty Good Privacy (PGP), 135
project management, 28
PROTECT algorithm, 104
provably secure cryptography, 80-82
pseudoscience, 10
The Pseudoscience Wars (Gordin), 10
public datasets, 34, 72, 94
public key infrastructure (PKI), 112
Pwn2Own contest, 103
PyVMI library, 102

Q

question formulation
  asking good questions, 15-18
  asking probing questions, 133
  for sales pitches, 164-166
Quist, Danny, 141

R

R software, 72, 116-118
RAID Symposium, 64
ranges (testbeds), 37
Reamde (Stephenson), 55
receiver operating characteristic (ROC) curve, 57-58
REcon Conference, 108
Recursive Feature Elimination (RFE), 50
regression analysis, 115-118
repeatability, 8, 93
reproducibility (scientific method), 8, 36, 93
results of experimentation
  analyzing, 21-24
  predictability of, 8
  sharing, 25
  situational awareness and, 68-70
Retrospective Probing technique, 133
Retrospective Think Aloud technique, 133
reverse engineering, 108
RFE (Recursive Feature Elimination), 50
rigor
  in incident response, 53
  scientific, 9
ROC (receiver operating characteristic) curve, 57-58
RSA Conference, 83
RStudio IDE, 72

S

sample sizes, 19
sandboxes, scientific data collection for, 100-102
Sandia National Laboratories, 46
satisfaction (usability), 130
scalability
  for intrusion detection, 58-60
  testing, 15
Schneier, Bruce, 77
Science of Security Virtual Organization (SoS VO), 10

scientific claims, 157, 160-162
scientific experiments, 42
  (see also cybersecurity experimentation)
  double-blind, 128
  in cryptography, 77-80
  in digital forensics, 89-90
  in intrusion detection, 54-55, 100
  in malware analysis, 100
  in situational awareness, 66-68
  in software assurance, 42-43
  in system security engineering, 113-115
  in usable security, 126-128
  in visualization, 142-144
scientific method
  about, 7
  cryptography and, 77
  elements of, 7, 15, 93
  Frye standard and, 91
  governing principles, 8
  motivations for, 6
  research methods supported, 8
  SDLC and, 45
scientific rigor, 9
SciStarter website, 102
Scott, David Meerman, 163
SDDR protocol, 78-78
SDLC (software development life cycle), 45
Security Architect job description, 83
security resource allocation, game theory for, 104
SecurityMetrics.org website, 13
Sen, Souyma, 60
Shannon, Claude, 80
Shneiderman, Ben, 131, 147
Sikorski, Michael, 99
Simon block ciphers, 83
simulation
  in test environments, 32-33
  scientific data collection for, 100-102
Siri speech recognition, 70
situational awareness
  big data and, 65
  finding needle in haystack, 73-75
  human network defenders and, 68-70
  network monitoring, 70-73
  scientific experiments in, 66-68
SLAM project, 44
The Sleuth Kit for Hadoop, 94
Snort intrusion detection package, 60-63

About the Author

Josiah Dykstra is a Senior Researcher at the Department of Defense. Dykstra received his PhD in Computer Science from the University of Maryland, Baltimore County, researching the technical and legal challenges of digital forensics for cloud computing. He is known in the DoD and forensics communities for his work on network security, intrusion detection, malware analysis, digital forensics, and cloud computing. He is a member of the ACM, IEEE, American Academy of Forensic Sciences, Cloud Security Alliance, and American Bar Association.

Colophon

The animal on the cover of *Essential Cybersecurity Science* is a Japanese rhinoceros beetle (*Allomyrina dichotoma*), also known as *kabutomushi* in Japanese—*mushi* for bug and *kabuto* for helmet (referring to a samurai helmet in this case).

The Japanese rhino beetle is distinct in its sexual dimorphism: males are much larger at 40–80 mm, whereas females reach about 40–60 mm. Males have a small thoracic horn and a longer cephalic horn with a characteristic Y shape, which they use during mating rituals and to maintain territory by lifting other males off the ground and tossing them into the air. This nocturnal species has white or red eyes that are adapted to low light levels. Both males and females have dark brown bodies with black ventral parts, and unusually long front legs. This species can be found in broad-leaved forests in tropical or subtropical mountainous environments in Japan, Taiwan, Korea, and eastern China. It feeds on tree sap, fruits, and generally sugary foods.

A Japanese rhino beetle spends most of its life underground, with only about four months spent as an actual beetle. It emerges from the ground in late spring, and usually dies in early fall after mating and laying eggs. Eggs are laid directly in the ground; once hatched into larva, offspring mature within a year. Males die after mating many times; female beetles usually die after laying eggs.

In Japan, many children buy or catch Japanese rhino beetles and breed them; these insects sell for about 500–1,000 yen (about $5–10). They are also very popular in gambling; in a popular game, two male beetles are placed on a log, where they battle, trying to push the other off the log. The sole beetle remaining on the log is the winner. Gambling over this game is a major source and loss of money, particularly in the Ryukyu Islands.

Many of the animals on O'Reilly covers are endangered; all of them are important to the world. To learn more about how you can help, go to *animals.oreilly.com*.

The cover image is from *Insects Abroad*. The cover fonts are URW Typewriter and Guardian Sans. The text font is Adobe Minion Pro; the heading font is Adobe Myriad Condensed; and the code font is Dalton Maag's Ubuntu Mono.

Get even more for your money.

Join the O'Reilly Community, and register the O'Reilly books you own. It's free, and you'll get:

- $4.99 ebook upgrade offer
- 40% upgrade offer on O'Reilly print books
- Membership discounts on books and events
- Free lifetime updates to ebooks and videos
- Multiple ebook formats, DRM FREE
- Participation in the O'Reilly community
- Newsletters
- Account management
- 100% Satisfaction Guarantee

Signing up is easy:

1. Go to: oreilly.com/go/register
2. Create an O'Reilly login.
3. Provide your address.
4. Register your books.

Note: English-language books only

To order books online:
oreilly.com/store

For questions about products or an order:
orders@oreilly.com

To sign up to get topic-specific email announcements and/or news about upcoming books, conferences, special offers, and new technologies:
elists@oreilly.com

For technical questions about book content:
booktech@oreilly.com

To submit new book proposals to our editors:
proposals@oreilly.com

O'Reilly books are available in multiple DRM-free ebook formats. For more information:
oreilly.com/ebooks

Lightning Source UK Ltd.
Milton Keynes UK
UKOW05f1614040318

318803UK00003B/5/P